China from the Inside Out

China from the Inside Out

Fitting the People's Republic into the World

RONALD C. KEITH

PLUTO PRESS
www.plutobooks.com

First published 2009 by Pluto Press
345 Archway Road, London N6 5AA and
175 Fifth Avenue, New York, NY 10010

www.plutobooks.com

Distributed in the United States of America exclusively by
Palgrave Macmillan, a division of St. Martin's Press LLC,
175 Fifth Avenue, New York, NY 10010

British Library Cataloguing in Publication Data
A catalogue record for this book is available from the British Library

ISBN   978 0 7453 2855 3   Hardback
ISBN   978 0 7453 2854 6   Paperback

Library of Congress Cataloging in Publication Data applied for

This book is printed on paper suitable for recycling and made from
fully managed and sustained forest sources. Logging, pulping and
manufacturing processes are expected to conform to the environmental
standards of the country of origin. The paper may contain up to
70 per cent post-consumer waste.

10 9 8 7 6 5 4 3 2 1

Designed and produced for Pluto Press by
Chase Publishing Services Ltd, Sidmouth, England
Typeset from disk by Stanford DTP Services, Northampton, England
Printed and bound in the European Union by
CPI Antony Rowe, Chippenham and Eastbourne

CONTENTS

ACKNOWLEDGEMENTS

I would like to thank my colleague, Professor Tareq Ismael, for suggesting that I write this book. Some of the book's interpretations and ideas were tried out on colleagues at the Griffith Asia Institute and China Policy Group, and their spirited rejoinders and views are very much appreciated. Also, I would like to acknowledge Chinese colleagues at Nankai University where I gave a recent keynote address at the Third International Symposium on Zhou Enlai Studies. Nankai Conference and seminar discussion helped me to think about the notion of a Chinese 'model' of international relations. The Social Sciences and Humanities Research Council of Canada has provided significant and sustained research funding over the years, and I have been able to incorporate some of the related findings into this book's analysis. Last, but certainly not least, I would like to thank Hou Shumei for her encouragement and also her help in fashioning the list of Chinese language concepts.

PREFACE

The former diplomat and grand historian of American China studies, John K. Fairbank, inaugurated the original Harvard regional studies area programme on China after 1946, and, at least since the 1951 first edition of his very popular *United States and China*,[1] there has been a plethora of books that have attempted to understand China. In fact over the decades several of these books specifically used the title, *Understanding China*.

As an undergraduate and masters student at the University of Toronto, I majored in history and took courses about China in 'East Asian Studies' that included a full range of courses in modern standard Chinese language and modern and classical Chinese literature. At that time in the early 1970s there was an already established and self-evidently reasonable, but as it turned out premature, assumption that area studies as it focused on Chinese history, culture and language could make a useful contribution to the understanding of contemporary China.

The dominant US area study of China had been developed in no small part as the result of the 1958 National Defense Education Act. The Act funded area studies as a matter of national strategic priority so as to ensure the creation of an appropriate education and knowledge base that would serve the American national interest against the spread of insurgency and revolution in the world. Also, the Act required a learning process and related curricular development that would more directly contribute to a better understanding of modern policy relevant issues. Likewise, in the UK, in 1959, Sir William Hayter reported that British university programmes had often exhibited the strong philological bias of classical 'Oriental' studies and that the universities needed to focus more clearly on the contemporary need to know about policy significant matters.[2]

The distinguished China expert John Lindbeck published in 1970 *Understanding China*. Essentially this book was a report for the Ford Foundation assessing the progress of US research on China. The National Defense Education Act and the subsequent development of China area studies, even if it was rationalized for deliberate strategic purposes, was arguably a contribution to understanding China. However, there were still problems. Lindbeck attempted to establish the importance of new China subject matter by arguing: '[China] is an inescapable and constant challenge to world understanding.' He claimed that China is 'more isolated than any other major nation' and that China's 'isolation is perplexing and anomalous'.[3]

The subject, and the study, of China was sometimes made to carry an extraneous political burden in the development of domestic American politics that was consumed by fierce disagreement over US involvement in Vietnam. Lindbeck was concerned about the purposes of American 'radically experimental social and political movements and anti-establishment groups'; however, his main point, as a public educator, was self-evident. In today's budgetary and curricular context it is well worth re-emphasizing the following point: 'Knowledge of the language is the necessary basis for the study of any society.'[4]

The very notion of the 'containment' of 'Red China' conjured up a biological metaphor of spreading disease. Such a metaphor did not argue for the rational understanding of China; and containment certainly did not facilitate the close-up study of changing China. In the early years, many Western China experts had no choice but to train outside China. Indeed, quite often they trained in Taiwan. However, it is argued herein that the PRC did not isolate itself for some unfathomable 'anomalous' reason. Containment was a distorted artefact of political purpose; and it was foisted on China as a new nation-state that was looking for recognition, based on principles of reciprocity and equality.

Containment facilitated loose generalizations about the aggressive nature of China as a mysterious 'Middle Kingdom'. Perhaps it also had the unintended consequence of keeping those engaged in the professional study of China, studying on China's periphery, looking eagerly from the outside in. Some younger Canadian, British and Australian scholars were able to make it to

Beijing for language studies in the 1970s. The Cold War dilemma of the China scholars was gradually alleviated in Sino-American normalization and with the development of Deng Xiaoping's 'open door' strategy in late 1978.

In 1977 I completed a doctoral dissertation on the early 1950s reintegration of national administration in China. The latter drew on an exceptionally rich collection of domestic Chinese documents; however, I went to China for the first time only in 1979. I participated in Beijing in a 9 May 1979 delegation discussion about the 1978 Amnesty International report, *Political Imprisonment of Prisoners in the People's Republic of China*.

Two leading Chinese academics from the Institute of Law, Chinese Academy of Social Sciences, Wu Daying and Zhang Zhonglin, then had the opportunity to respond directly to the reported claims of Amnesty International; however, in the course of discussing Chinese interpretation of 'judicial independence' and 'equality before the law', they made it clear that the current legal reform was largely a matter of 'restoring' many 'reasonable' laws that had been created prior to the Cultural Revolution. Moreover it was asserted that any new legal structures would be put in place under the custodial leadership of the Party and that in their view, legal institutions were not designed for the sole purpose of challenging the leadership of the Chinese Communist Party.[5]

John Bryan Starr's first words in his updated edition of *Understanding China* were: 'To the limited extent that Westerners pay attention to what is going on beyond their shores, China commands a disproportionate share of that attention.' Starr described the initial American euphoria in the 1980s for Deng Xiaoping's open door and economic reform. In the mid 1980s, admiration of Deng and his new policy direction had 'the unintended effect of filtering out much of the bad news'. Indeed, the focus was on the road to market reform and not Deng Xiaoping's 'four cardinal principles', *sixiang jiben yuanze*, that supported Party leadership and institutions as against the spread of 'bourgeois liberalization'.

It was not until the apparent wake-up call in Tiananmen Square in 1989 and the subsequent collapse of the Soviet Union in 1991 that there was an extraordinary shift in the American attitude towards China. These momentous events drew everyone's attention to the apparently intractable nature of the Party State, and the international media rigorously devoted almost all of its attention to China's lack of progress in governance, democracy and human rights development.[6]

Arguably, the negative featuring of the Chinese regime thereafter influenced opinion on the implications of China's contemporary 'rise'. As China plunged to the bottom of the freedom charts in the West, China studies and area studies more generally came under increasing attack from the social sciences, particularly from political science and economics. It is a profound paradox that in the era of globalization, language studies were underfunded as they were regarded as an expensive and somewhat superfluous distraction from core curricula.

With the advent of reform and China's open door since December 1978 one might have expected that the 'understanding' of China would have gotten at least more easy if not more sophisticated in its critical balance. From the 1990s to the present, China area studies, however, have continued to decline despite intense international focus on China's 'rise' and despite 'realist' warnings of the China threat underwritten by China's apparent growing economic power. China is now in the world and the world is in China, and yet the formal study of China still has to contend with so much recycled myth and hyperbole. The social sciences reduced China area studies in the context of often oversimplified media hyperbole and uninformed political speculation about China's real intentions in the world. Speculation about China has become a cottage industry for a growing array of pundits, many of whom are unable to use sources in the Chinese language.

None other than the author of the thesis on the 'end of history', Francis Fukuyama, came to the defence of ailing area studies. As a top educator/administrator at the School of Advanced International Studies, Fukuyama explained that while there may have been some truth to the often repeated argument that area studies had become too 'parochial and overspecialized', there had been unnecessarily concerted institutional efforts to reduce area studies and cultural-historical inquiry in favour of 'objective', quantifiable social science:

> ...regional studies fell seriously out of favor in the 1980s and 1990s. Foundations ceased to fund area studies programs, money for language training and fieldwork evaporated and requirements were changed from knowing languages and history to learning quantitative methods. Regional studies requires a huge personal investment, not just in specialized training but also in having to live in a particular country and building up a network of contacts to keep one's knowledge fresh throughout a career....[7]

The current book reasserts the importance of China area studies to the study of salient policy issues; and it will once more take up the task of understanding the critical contemporary issues concerning governance, the rule of law, human rights and democracy and their relation to peace and development and what is called the 'China threat'. In the first place, the analysis deliberately proceeds on the basis of an area studies protocol that moves from the inside out, identifying and assessing the conclusions of the formal learning process that is used internally to explain China's place in the world.

Secondly, the analysis focuses on the developing Chinese dialectical response to key Western ideas and institutions that have been assigned 'Chinese characteristics'. Paradoxically, most of the key constructs such as democracy, human rights, the rule of law, globalization, development, the 'socialist' market, the 'China threat', even Marxism-Leninism, are Western in origin. Obviously, the nature and scope of the Chinese process that attaches 'Chinese characteristics' (*Zhongguo tesede*) to such foreign values, institutions and ideas is important to any serious analysis of the interaction between China and the outside world.

The Chinese have done a considerable amount of often unrecognized thinking as to how to learn about these concepts and as to how they might be practically used to fit China into the world. In my visits to Beijing's top research institutes and centres I often encountered an explicitly stated Chinese belief in the importance of learning as the basis for advancing national economic development. And indeed any discussion about matters of security and 'threat' was always premised in the unity of domestic and international considerations. Related policy dialectics invariably cast security as derivative of development.

Chinese analysis has professed a certain frustration that the Western media and scholarship have shown such a spectacular lack of interest in the Chinese interpretation of Chinese priorities and policy assumptions. If recognized, the latter is often treated exclusively as an artful but less than substantive matter of Chinese deception. And as for governance, the Chinese for their part have repeated many times that the core issue is meeting the needs of the Chinese people as opposed to complying with the externally dictated requirements of the critics in Amnesty International or in the US Congress.

There are basic differences of interpretation, but when area studies investigates the internal viewpoint and rationalization, this is not necessarily a matter of cultural relativism. China area studies can provide legitimate occasion for considering local political, economic and socio-cultural variables that contribute to a wider and more informed explanation of how one of the world's largest societies and oldest civilizations is now connecting with the outside world.

China's politicians and scholars are talking about 'facing modernization, facing the world, and facing the future' (*mianxiang xiandaihua, mianxiang shijie, mianxiang weilai*). The Chinese Communist Party (CCP) is now placing greater emphasis on political reform and is also currently much more interested in China's ancient civilization than before. There is less reference to the 'sinification of Marxism-Leninism' (*Zhongguohuade MakesiLieningzhuyi*), but there is now a more deliberately encompassing discourse on how contemporary China is a product of the near and deep past as it faces the future.

The 'past' is no longer so exclusively focused on a history of dynastic rebellion that leads to modern revolution. In the author's own work, this became evident for example in the changing interpretation of the diplomacy of Zhou Enlai. When I published *The Diplomacy of Zhou Enlai* in 1989, political controversy over Zhou Enlai, as a latter-day Confucian, was still relatively recent.

The extreme leftist class politics of the Cultural Revolution had caricatured Zhou as a Confucian 'reactionary', and with the advent of Deng Xiaoping's reform era, such deliberate vilification was discounted with the attack on the Gang of Four. The campaigns against Confucius have since stopped, whereas the Confucian preference for peace as opposed to militarism is increasingly celebrated. Today, it is much easier to research Mao Zedong as a Daoist dialectician, and to discuss how Zhou's five principles and his operational strategy of 'seeking common ground while reserving differences' resonate with the Confucian emphasis on 'harmony with differences'.[8]

Internal discourse and related policy and institutional change ought to be rolled into a wider informed understanding of China. Such discourse, for example, not only offers a deliberate and convincing rebuttal to the assumptions underlying the so-called 'China Threat', but also offers new thinking as to the composition of, and the contemporary political and economic interactions within, the world order as the latter concern non-traditional threats to security and economic crisis.

Arguably, it is important not to lose the opportunities presented in a Chinese viewpoint that espouses on the basis of the original five principles of peaceful coexistence an alternative world order that newly-emphasizes 'democratized international relations' and the 'diversity of civilizations' and that re-emphasizes diplomacy rather than pre-emptive force and unilateral military force in favour of notions of common security and development.

For a long time now, area studies had little direct access to China. The Chinese Communists, however, had the habit of deliberately explaining themselves to the world. In the context of containment this was done, for example, through people's diplomacy and foreign-language press publications. This trend has become more routinized, and, since the early 1990s, there was a flurry of 'White Papers' that with more international documentation and somewhat less ideological jargon convey the official Chinese viewpoint on what is happening in China. Taken together, these White Papers constitute a new level of regular recorded response to Western criticisms of China's authoritarian politics and human rights violations.[9] Such documentation is indeed subjective but it is also analytically interesting in its explanations of internal perspectives and in its direct response to international criticism.

There remains one final note. The current Chinese civilizational notion of *he er butong* (harmony without uniformity) is about an essentially political element of reciprocity and equality that must be operationalized in mutual learning processes that interpret the potential for common purpose in the context of the changing realities of world politics. Fairbank might well have approved of a viewpoint that deliberately features 'harmony without uniformity', as he wrote in the 1983 preface of his fourth edition: 'Our hope must be that a mutual understanding of our discordant motivation can help us accept our differences.'[10]

1

UNDERSTANDING CHINA ONCE MORE

In today's world the mere mention of 'China' is likely to invoke the notion of 'rise'. Many books have offered an understanding of China. Scholars, pundits and policy-makers have provided conflicting and sometimes sensationalized opinions on the nature of the Chinese state and society and on the Chinese view of war and peace and the related implications of China's rise.

The Chinese, in their own review of China's place in the world, have, themselves, debated the connotations of 'peaceful rise' (*heping jueqi*). Despite the qualifying reference to 'peace', they opted to avoid this particular expression for fear that any reference to 'rising' at all would create regional and international anxiety over the 'China Threat' (*Zhongguo weixie*).

On occasion pundits such as Charles Krauthammer have responded to China's rise, calling for the reinstatement of the 'containment' of China in US foreign policy. Despite China's 'opening', there is a great deal of obfuscation about China's real intentions, and informed understanding of relevant Chinese policy and strategy is at a very great premium. For this reason, this book's thematic narrative attempts once more to understand China's adaptation to the modern world, paying special attention to the current hot controversies concerning human rights, the rule of law, democracy, the Chinese development of 'socialism' and China's related 'rise' in international relations.

The Comparative Dilemma of 'Wealth and Power'

During the last several decades of the nineteenth century and the first decades of the twentieth, Chinese nationalists focused on creating the state's 'wealth and power' (*fuqiang*). This particular focus was a reflection of the international state system, but it may have caused some underlying Western concern as to whether Chinese nationalism would ultimately turn aggressive. Certainly, the key notion of 'wealth and power' conflicted with the extant principles underlying the Chinese imperium and ultimately undermined the Chinese own world view. Nationalism that was filliped in the anguish of humiliating defeat at the hands of the great powers, including Japan, as China's former 'tributary', ultimately called into question the relevance of the Confucian ordering of the state within a moral universe in which the relations between princes was governed by the same principles governing the relations between family members.

As China's weakness was exposed in the spread of colonialism and loss of sovereignty, the brutal implications became clear enough in China and in the region. The obvious military superiority of the great powers and the cultural threat of Western civilization posed a common problem for many of the countries in nineteenth-century Asia. In terms of the response to the West, the issues often boiled down to how to change and just how much change is necessary to meet the external threat. The option of outright self-seclusion was often initially seen as preferable to making any cultural concessions to the outside world. This option was tried in Japan and Korea whereas China attempted to keep the foreign presence far down the southern coast; but with the expansion of imperialism, self-seclusion was no longer a practical response to the pressures of change coming from the outside world.

A brief comparison of the Chinese and Japanese responses reveals the different pathways that were taken in the response to the West. Within an official context of seclusion, foreign learning was often viewed as subversive in nature, but the advocates of 'Dutch Learning' persisted in their efforts to expand the knowledge of Western science in late Tokugawa Japan. Sakuma Shozan (1811–1864), for example, justified his interest in Western gunnery by advocating the rather ethereal notion of 'Eastern Ethics and Western Science'.[1] In 1853–54 US Commodore Mathew Perry literally forced open Japan's door to trade and European style diplomatic relations. Unlike the Chinese who were remarkably steady and sedate in their carefully orchestrated relations with the foreign 'barbarian', the Japanese swiftly moved from a position of self-seclusion to a wide-open learning process that would facilitate the recovery of Japan's rights vis-à-vis the great powers. In 1868, the Meiji Emperor had his followers proclaim a Charter Oath of Five Articles, the last articles of which explicitly promised to abandon 'base customs of former times' and to seek knowledge 'throughout the world' so as to strengthen the 'foundation of the imperial polity'.[2] This was followed by a remarkable top-down process of political centralization which in the 1870s witnessed the collapse of the daimyo system, the disarming of the samurai and the advent of national conscription.

Japanese society and politics were irrevocably changed. The issue of how to adapt went far beyond the question as to how to acquire Western gunnery. There were intense crazes over Western things followed by the robust reassertion of Japanese values; nevertheless, the extent to which the Japanese considered the need to change society and key institutions in a fundamental way was truly remarkable.

One of Japan's greatest educators, Fukuzawa Yukichi, for example, wrote in 1871 of the ignorance of both the Chinese and the Japanese as to the central importance of liberty and the corresponding need to introduce a radical notion of equality into familial relations:

> ...it is a peculiar characteristic of human beings that they have the ability to secure liberty of mind and of actions.... It is right that the father and the child, the master and retainer, and the husband and wife should all have this liberty.... When every individual, every family, and every province, shall obtain this liberty, then, and not till then, can we expect to witness the true independence of the nation....[3]

Such viewpoints challenged head-on the apparently benighted Confucian notion of 'filial piety'.

The difference in the scope and speed of Japanese and Chinese responses to the West may be partly explained in the structural differences of their respective Confucian experience. In Japan,

Confucianism was conscripted from abroad and grafted on to a native understanding of society that celebrated *bushido*, or the 'way of the warrior'.[4] These reconstituted Confucian values were later easily coopted into the rationalization of Japanese militarism. In China, Confucianism was indigenous and thoroughgoing. Confucianism served as the principal element of a deliberately syncretic tradition that based itself upon an essentially civil principle of moral government as opposed to the 'way of the hegemon'.

The Chinese Confucian tradition optimistically assumed that there is a latent good in all and that goodness is immanent in the cosmos. The *wang* character, in the 'kingly way' (*wangdao*), for example, included one vertical stroke linking in the moral personality of the king, three levels of meaning pertaining to the earth, man and heaven. The Confucian way was impressively universal in its assumption of the moral potential of all those living within the four seas, but it presumed the importance of moral hierarchy that naturally reinforces harmony in the family and society. Confucianism required that everyone had to keep to their respective positions in society and that those who were able to cultivate their inner morality were naturally entitled to rule others who would be awed by their moral example. Neither in China nor in Japan did Confucianism offer ready support for the essential equality that animates modern Western notions of citizenship and representative government.

In the Chinese case the threat of the West was initially downplayed. There was an enervating complacency in the view that China had been conquered in the past only to re-emerge as a great civilization that had on many occasions converted its foreign enemies to the unique moral superiority of the Chinese way. In dealing with foreign threats imperial tactics usually focused on the acquisition of outside superior technology. This was facilitated in the selective assimilation of Western experts into imperial service. At the same time in the mid nineteenth century the court and its supporters in the regions fostered a notion of 'self-strengthening'. In essence this was a kind of moral re-armament of Confucian officials who needed to re-focus on providing moral example in good governance.

Comparatively late in the nineteenth century Zhang Zhidong provided the closest parallel to the Japanese notion of 'Eastern Ethics and Western Science' when he elaborated on 'Eastern learning as essence, Western learning as use' (use meaning technology and science), *zhongxue wei ti, xixue wei yong.*

Zhang had originally responded to the West with a purist position within the Spring Purification Circle at court that simply called for the elimination of the contaminating influence of Western civilization on China. Once Zhang witnessed humiliating defeat in the Sino-French War of 1885 he moved to the more 'progressive' position of using Western science, technology and military hardware and training to protect China's inner 'essence'.

Zhang went a step further when in 1898 he published *China's Only Hope*, exhorting the scholar literati to learn new things only in order to protect extant civilization:

> ...there are three things necessary to be done in order to save China from revolution. The first is to maintain the reigning Dynasty; the second is to conserve the holy religion, and the third is to protect the Chinese race.... in order to protect the Chinese race we must first conserve the religion, and if the religion is to be conserved we are bound to maintain the dynasty. But, it may be asked, how can we protect the Race? We reply, by knowledge, and knowledge is religion; and religion is propagated by strength, and strength lies in troops.[5]

In 1903, in a petulant burst of nationalist angst, Zou Rong wrote a much different kind of tract calling for the killing of the Qing emperor. This was Zou's way of protecting the 'race'. Zou wanted China to become a republic because he wanted China to be strong, and he wanted the Han people to throw off the yoke of the foreign Qing. Moreover, he believed that the existing scholarly elite had utterly failed to 'learn' what China actually needed; hence, in a fit of arrogant petulance he denounced the stupidity of the people and the scholars: 'Chinese scholars certainly have hardly a breath of life in them. Why is this so? The people are stupid because they do not learn, the literati are stupid, then they learn things they should not learn, and are the more stupid for it.'[6]

Zou denounced the reigning non-Han dynasty, the Qing, as a 'furry race'. Not only were their hearts 'beast's hearts', but their customs were 'the customs of the users of wool'. Such 'racist' commentary reflected the prevailing social Darwinism circulating in China's treaty ports. Zou's enthusiastic, if not fierce ambition for China was explicit in the following judgement: '...China is capable of embracing the whole world, of shaking and dazzling the entire globe, or surveying benignly the nations from its heights and dominating the five continents.'[7]

The Confucian notion of the 'Middle Kingdom', *Zhongguo*, had for centuries characterized China as a universal empire whose moral civilization stretched between 'the four seas'. This notion did not survive what the father of modern China, Sun Yatsen, called 'hypocolonialism'. According to Sun, India only had to contend with the British, but in China several great powers competed for China's resources and territory, carving out their own spheres of influence wherein Chinese law and jurisdiction was so obviously disrespected. Modern Chinese nationalism went through this stressful birthing and it was unable to reconcile with any past cultural notion of China as a universal empire.

Writing in 1926, an American professor, who had been involved in the crafting of a new state constitution for President Yuan Shikai, attempted what might be regarded, despite its occasional rhetorical licence, as a rather informed and self-consciously multidimensional explanation of the cultural and the political economic contradictions underlying the dazed Chinese response to the West:

> In the economic situation in which Europe was 600 years ago, China was called upon almost at once to transform herself. With pacifist traditions centuries old she was required to meet the arbitrary exactions of militaristic powers. Drugged with the narcotic of a quietist philosophy, she was asked to guide her footsteps along the pathway of the strenuous life. Accustomed to think in terms of the family, she was called upon to organize her social *life in* a way which seemed to her immoral. With an admiration for literary

accomplishment which has never been elsewhere excelled, she was brought face to face with a world in which literary culture was being forced to give way to scientific and technical studies. No wonder the Chinese were dazed both by the strangeness of the demands made upon them and by the violence by which these demands were accompanied. For a time they stood stupefied like men awakened from a sound sleep. It was some time before they were able to comprehend their situation.[8]

If he was aware of the perilous road ahead, Professor Goodnow still concluded that the 'fundamental strength of the Chinese character' would prevail. While others feared that China would become a future threat. Referring to the future resurrection of the Chinese character, Goodnow concluded: 'When that happens *China will arise*, which will present to the world the spectacle of a well ordered land.' In his view, the Chinese would ultimately eschew 'aggressive nationalism' and would resume the task of 'contributing to other peoples of the earth'.[9]

'Nationalism' and 'Cosmopolitanism'

The founding father of the modern Chinese nation-state, Sun Yatsen was not quite as concerned about China's future contribution to other peoples as he was concerned about China's immediate survival. Anxious to protect the young roots of Chinese nationalism, Sun decried the evils of 'cosmopolitanism' (*shijiezhuyi*) that came in two different forms, one traditional Chinese, the other modern Anglo-American.

In the first place, Sun Yatsen critiqued China's past 'theory of world empire' as a contemporary liability that distracted attention away from Chinese nationalism as a good, in and of itself. Sun reasoned: 'Before China was subjugated she thought she was situated at the moral centre of the world and so named herself the "Middle Kingdom".' Sun viewed persisting Middle Kingdom-ism as a regressive cosmopolitanism. Noting that 'nationalism is that precious possession by which humanity maintains its existence', he warned that should the Chinese people embrace 'cosmopolitanism': 'We will be unable to survive and will be eliminated by other races.' In effect Sun was saying do not let the Chinese empire stand in the way of the modern Chinese nation.

Secondly, Sun warned of a deceptive external form of 'cosmopolitanism'. He warned of the blandishments of the British and Americans: 'The nations that are employing imperialism to conquer others and which are trying to maintain their own favoured positions as sovereign lords of the whole world are advocating cosmopolitanism and want the world to join them.'[10]

In commentary which invokes the contemporary fascination with 'Chinese characteristics', Sun also discussed the relation between China's own particular characteristics and 'modern world tendencies' including those relating to democracy:

> For thousands of years Chinese social sentiments, customs, and habits have differed widely from those of Western society. Hence methods of social control in China are different from those used in the West and we should not merely copy the West as we copy the use of their machinery. ...The West has its society; we have our society, and the sentiments and customs of the two are not the same. Only as we adapt ourselves, according to our social conditions, to modern world tendencies, can we hope to reform our society and to advance our nation. If we pay no attention to our own social conditions and try simply to follow world tendencies, our nation will decline and our people will be in peril. If we want China to progress and our race to be safe, we must put democracy into effect ourselves and do some radical thinking about the best way to realize its ideals.[11]

Especially when it came to the organization of the fundamental institutions of government, Sun had the same kind of strong reservation against mechanical copying of foreign experience as Mao Zedong.

In the early 1940s, Jiang Meiling Song, wife of Chiang Kai-shek and a roving ambassador of goodwill in the US, was searching for words so as to explain the road that China must take. Mme Song settled on one Latin word that she had found incised in the southern portal of St Paul's Cathedral in London – '*Resurgam*'.[12] For the average parishioner this term might have evoked Christ's rise from the dead, but for Mme Song, it symbolically synthesized the wisdom of East and West in China's future. *Resurgam* invoked

'The spirit that is China.' In reflecting on this 'spirit', Mme Song quoted Socrates' injunction to his students: 'Know thyself.'

Socrates might well have approved of the ancient Chinese aphorism attributed to Sun-tzu, *zhi ji zhi bi* ('know yourself and know your enemy').[13] Today's foreign policy focus on 'harmony' originates with Confucian assumptions. Certainly an inclusive review of the Chinese perspective on war and peace has to take into account Confucian contempt for militarism as both morally bankrupt and economically inefficient. In the Confucian tradition, knowing the self, or 'cultivating the self' (*xiu shen*) is critical as it leads to the harmonious development of moral relations in the family and society and eventually to 'peace' for 'all under heaven', *tianxia*. This is how to understand the famous aphorism, *xiu shen, qi jia, zhi guo, tianxia ping*, or 'cultivate the self, regulate the family, rule the kingdom and there will be peace under heaven'.[14]

Within this continuum the state is the moral extension of society. It does not exist for its own independent purposes of raising taxes and fighting wars, and, if states were to be 'rightly governed', then there would be no need of war between kingdoms. Harmony at the universal level is to become manifest in the relations between princes based on '*li*' (decorum). Both domestic and international rulership was rooted in '*xiao*' or filial piety, hence the expression, *yi xiao zhi tianxia*, 'with filial piety rule all under heaven'. Accordingly, the best guarantee of security in society is the popular belief in the moral righteousness of the social order.

A society that is morally well ordered will naturally defend itself. A morally contented population serves as a strong deterrent against any outside threat, hence the following celebrated logic: 'Therefore the master conqueror does not fight; the expert warrior needs no soldiers; the truly great commander requires not to set his troops in battle array.'[15] Unfortunately Chinese nationalism developed in a world shaped by combative imperialisms where admonitions to 'knowing thyself' were not enough to save a nation. In this world, 'righteousness' was apparently the last refuge of the weak and commitment to '*li*' meaning profit was far more important than social relations governed by decorum, or ritual, (*li*). But the really important question then is: Did Chinese nationalism become aggressive in its adaptation to a world politics driven by profit and war?

However, Mme Song, a devout Christian, put together an interest in Western institutions and values with an honest and self-critical wisdom gleaned from China's ancient civilization: 'To build a strong, unified China it behooves us all to engage in intensive introspection, to be scrupulously honest in our estimate of our past shortcomings, and to acknowledge frankly our past mistakes with a view to correcting them in future.' Mme Song somewhat prematurely concluded: 'As a foundation for all this we have our ancient culture; as a goal we have free constitutional government, upon the threshold of which we are now.'[16]

Some nationalists were completely beyond 'intense introspection'. They discarded everything Chinese to save China from being 'carved up like a melon'. Others went to the opposite extreme claiming 'Everything Chinese is best' (*guocuizhuyi*). And then there were the young Marxist-Leninist nationalists who were looking for a new material explanation of why China was so weak in the face of the military and technical superiority of overweening great powers.

The mentor of Mao Zedong, Li Dazhao, rebuked the co-founder of the Chinese Communist Party, Chen Duxiu, for having too little faith in the Chinese people and culture: 'We ought not to stop thinking about our country and refuse to love it because the country has deficiencies.'[17] Li came up with an idea that later especially appealed to Mao Zedong's nationalist sense of revolution, namely, that China's very weakness provided an opportunity to leap into the future. In Li's voluntarist viewpoint, because of its very backwardness China could stride the world stage as a 'proletarian nation'.

Such revolutionary nationalist sentiment in a sense liberated China from constraining notions such as the Asian mode of production or oriental despotism, both of which saw China stuck in history failing to move forward due to the intransigent everlasting socio-economic contradictions of a strong state and widely scattered self-sufficient village economy.

Mao Zedong as China's Paradox

On the issue of nationalism, history, culture and power, Li's protégé, Mao, was one of the most influential and, notwithstanding his penchant for revolutionary rhetoric, sophisticated observers of China's predicament. While Mao disavowed iconoclasts, he had no time for those traditionalists who would 'use the past against the present' (*yigu fei jin* or *gu wei jin yong*). As a 'pragmatic' Chinese nationalist and a revolutionary, he looked for ways for the 'past to serve the present' (*yigu wei jin*). On the other hand, Mao, the historian, claimed: '…we must respect our own history and must not lop it off'. Not surprisingly, Mao intensely disliked 'wholesale westernization'.

Although he had not travelled abroad, Mao was very open to learning about 'foreign progressive culture'. In 1940 he stated a position that moved beyond that of the Zhang Zhidong *ti-yong* strategy and became increasingly important after 1949:

> To nourish her own culture China needs to assimilate a good deal of foreign progressive culture, not enough of which was done in the past. We should assimilate whatever is useful to us today not only from the present-day socialist and new-democratic cultures but also from the earlier cultures of other nations, for example, from the culture of the various capitalist countries in the Age of Enlightenment.[18]

Mao wanted to use his newly acquired Marxist science of dialectics to distil the good and bad of the Chinese and all other culture on the basis of a theory of contradictions that celebrated 'seeking the truth from the facts' (*shishi qiu shi*). This key saying later became the credo of Deng Xiaoping in the post-1978 era of economic reform and the open door.

Mao's paradox was China's paradox. Like Zou, he displayed a frightening chiliastic rhetoric. When it came to learning within the internal confines of Party policy-making, however, he deferred to science. He was not, in Goodnow's language, the victim of a 'quietist philosophy'. He was deliberately modest in his approach to learning. This modesty identified and reflected upon the limits of China's development. Scaling the heights and at one and the same time 'seeking the truth from the facts' was not an easy task.

The persistence of mistakes in early Chinese revolutionary praxis confirmed the importance of modesty as the content of truth became progressively more relative. The formal adjustment to mistakes was based on a Party workstyle of direct inductive investigation and criticism and self-criticism. For Mao and his Party this workstyle was quintessentially 'scientific'. Mao's Chinese modesty likely informed his Marxist material dialectics. 'Truth' was not the absolute word of a 'Son of Heaven', or of a solitary sage in a temple hall. It was a down-to-earth business of collective debates that worked its way through the never-ending grind of contradictory social and economic developments.

Mao had once observed: 'All of us without exception must study.' Study and the investigation of things were essential to finding better policy, and mistakes along the way were inevitable and quite useful. In a rare self-criticism, Mao elaborated using a traditional metaphorical explanation of solar and lunar eclipses:

> The faults of the superior man are like the eclipses of the sun and moon. ...we see that even Confucius made mistakes, so we must conclude that all men without exception make some mistakes, more or fewer, bigger or smaller. It doesn't matter if we make mistakes, we must not let mistakes become a burden to us, we mustn't see them as something extraordinary, we should just go ahead and correct them.... It's like the celestial dog eats the sun and the moon – he makes a mistake, and everyone sees it. When he corrects his mistake, 'all men look up' to him.[19]

Hence the Party's mass line was deliberately rooted in a collective and experiential wisdom that fostered regular 'criticism and self-criticism' and was captured in the Party's essential distinction between the traditional 'one person temple' (yi yan tang) and the 'all-the-people-speak temple' (qun yan tang). In the latter case there was more room for creativity and for the admission of mistakes as a guide to learning.

Whereas Mao spoke of the crucial significance of politics in engaging the Chinese people in his revolution, in a public speech in 1948 the famous American writer, Pearl S. Buck (Sai Zhenzhu), spoke of the transience of government. She refused to offer her opinion on the vital question of the day as to whether the Communists were actually 'agrarians' (i.e., nationalists who were interested in enhancing Chinese agriculture, but were not interested in Communism). She said that she would not talk about politics 'because I do not consider it fundamental to China's people'. In a manner that suggests Goodnow's earlier view on the strength of the Chinese character, Pearl Buck did express her passionate belief in the destiny of the Chinese people:

> I have absolute confidence in the Chinese. They have lived long and they have weathered everything long ago, even Communism. They exist, though their contemporaries in Greece and Rome have gone. They do not believe in aggressive war because they have too much common sense. They live, and have lived longer than any people have ever lived, with the possible exception of the people of India. They are not weak, they are not decadent. China's people upon the land are strong and resilient and practical. Nothing can destroy them. Only folly can ignore them, only stupidity and ignorance can despise them.[20]

Containment and the Persistence of Realism

Subsequent containment of 'Red China' was indeed borne of just such folly, if not stupidity, but then, as will be described in Chapter 2, Cold War containment provided the new Chinese leaders with the dialectical opportunity to make a virtue out of a negative condition. In their response to the limitations of containment, they created a highly effective approach to international relations that has been sustained down to this day even in the contemporary era of 'globalization'.

The founding of the People's Republic of China (PRC) occasioned ugly recriminations in American politics. In the vitriolic attacks of Senator McCarthy on the US State Department, leading government China experts were accused of being 'Communists', themselves, just for merely suggesting that the Chinese in their nationalism might be detached from the leadership of Moscow. Any 'lobbying' for recognition served as a demonstration of communist conspiracy as rightwing extremists hunted for those who had 'lost China'.

Admiral Arthur W. Radford, in his foreword to the 1963 book by Robert Hunter and Forrest Davis, *The Red China Lobby*, did not, to use Pearl Buck's words, 'ignore' the Chinese but he fully wanted to 'destroy' their threat to the free world. He insisted that China's recognition would comfort the enemies of the free world. He believed that the US was involved in a 'war', 'understood in its broadest application – the struggle for victory by all available means, political, economic and subversive as well as military'. Radford was categorical: 'Red China intends to rule the Western Pacific and subjugate all of the Asias outside the Soviet empire.'

Despite the subsequent Sino-US normalization and the post-1978 development of open door and economic reform that in its recent stages have witnessed China's dynamic participation in globalization, the fundamental issue of Chinese motivation is still hotly contested in the anachronistic hyperbole of the 'China Threat'. The Cold War has come and gone, there is no longer a 'Red China', and China now participates in globalization with great effect, but the issue of a 'China Threat' has, nevertheless, been resurrected. This is the case even though the Chinese distinctions between 'capitalism' and 'socialism' have become extraordinarily ambiguous and even though no one seriously expects the PRC, which is now only in the 'primary stage of socialism' to lead an international movement to Communism any time soon.

After so much sophisticated adaptation on the Chinese part to the world, the extreme rhetoric of aggressive intent is still featured in the contemporary 'realist' rhetoric concerning the 'China Threat'. While the putative peace-loving tendency of China's ancient civilization is increasingly stressed in contemporary Chinese foreign policy, no serious major figure or Chinese leader since 1915 has tried to reinstate the Chinese empire as a 'Middle Kingdom', and the historical record of post-1949 Chinese foreign policy has continuously stressed equality and reciprocity between states.

Apparently, China is still a threat largely because it is not a liberal democracy like the US. Even though original Cold War containment was a significant policy failure in its unrealistic and uniformed assumptions about the realities of China and the world, the failed notion of 'containment' is still embraced by realists. In his well known 31 July 1995 *Time* essay, Charles Krauthammer, for example, argued that 'the aggressively dictatorial regime' in Beijing had to be contained. Claiming that 'containment' was not a Cold War invention but a legitimate age-old 'principle of power politics', he demanded that 'containment of such a bully' had to begin immediately.[21] Deng Xiaoping, of course, thought that the real 'bully' in the room was the US and that at any rate 'power politics' was not an acceptable basis for the conduct of modern international relations.

In 2000, Steven Mosher started his book on China with a rather extraordinary statement: 'The role of the Hegemon is deeply embedded in China's national dreamwork, intrinsic to its national identity, and profoundly implicated in its sense of national destiny.'[22] Mosher saw President Clinton's 'strategic partnership' as 'a direct descendant of Kissinger's promiscuous embrace of Zhou Enlai'.

While one might question Goodnow's use of 'pacifism' to explain the Chinese character, there is an obviously strong bias against militarism in the Chinese tradition. Mosher drew on the ancient Chinese idea of '*ba*', as in *baquanzhuyi*, or 'hegemony'. The appearance of this term apparently confirms that the Chinese invented 'totalitarianism' 2,800 years ago. Mosher did not stop there. He claimed that since Tiananmen Square in 1989 the Chinese have been practising an extreme form of cultural superiority: 'The keepers of state orthodoxy...have lately seized upon what I think of as Great Han chauvinism (*da Zhonghuazhuyi*): a potent and peculiarly Chinese combination of nationalism, ultrapatriotism, traditionalism, ethnocentrism and culturalism.'[23]

The modern Chinese insistence that 'China shall never seek hegemony' relates to the denial of Chinese sovereignty by US imperialism. The same reasoning underlines contemporary Chinese support for the recognition of the 'diversity of civilizations'. Mosher ignores this altogether. The association of the Chinese with 'hegemonism' verges on casuistry in light of the mainstream Confucian disdain for *badao* (the 'way of the hegemon'), as it is distinguished from the morally superior *wangdao* (the 'way of the king'). The latter's legitimacy presumed 'sageliness within, kingliness without', meaning that the latent good inside the ruler becomes manifest in his exemplary relations with people in society. This is essentially a good governance that generates security inside and outside any kingdom. The 'way of the king' was predicated in the development of moral civilization whereas the 'way of the hegemon' was associated with brute force.[24] Of course, modern day Chinese analysis does associate the latter with American 'realism'.

As more fully described in Chapter 2, the Chinese response to containment and exclusion from the UN did not take the form of aggressive nationalist resort to power politics. This was the case despite tremendous Cold War provocation. Instead the Chinese deployed a highly effective diplomacy that deliberately eschewed 'hegemony' against the American alliance system. It was against this kind of backdrop that the Chinese kept repeating the formulation: 'China will never seek hegemony.'

The interpretation of China's 'rise' is a patently risky business, but an area studies reading of Chinese culture and history can contribute to a more informed understanding of China. Chinese learning sometimes challenges tradition, while at other times the Chinese past is self-consciously confirmed as relevant to China's present and future.

In providing such a reading there are still going to be significant points of contention. The analysis herein, for example, not only disputes realist claims as to the China threat but challenges John Lindbeck's assumption that China's 'isolation is perplexing and anomalous'.[25] The Chinese did not isolate themselves. Containment required a lot of work on the part of others. Even so, the protracted Chinese response was not to build a challenging pro-Beijing military alliance, but politically to undermine containment on the basis of a rational inclusive diplomatic strategy. And it is very important to note that while they dealt with containment, the Chinese went through an important formal process of learning that directly addressed questions as to how China, in its goals of peace and development, would fit into the world.

2

FITTING THE PEOPLE'S REPUBLIC OF CHINA INTO THE WORLD

As for fitting the People's Republic of China (PRC) into the world, there are several related questions that require further understanding. How did the new Chinese nation state fit into a world essentially characterized by the epic Cold War struggle between the two social systems of 'socialism' and 'capitalism'? To achieve the primary goal of national economic development the Chinese Communist Party (CCP) had to find a way of taking China out into the world. As nationalists the CCP leaders wanted recognition for their nation-state, but not at any price. As Chinese Marxist-Leninists they hoped, on the basis of China's independence and self-reliance, to promote national economic development and domestic social progress while participating in the international division of labour and eventually gaining foreign aid and technology on the basis of reciprocity and equality.

China's new leaders were not interested in autarchy, but they were very interested in finding a way to break out of US-led containment. What happened to Chinese nationalism as it was spawned in a domestic struggle for revolution and in the international context of containment? China was flatly denied international acceptance. The US worked against acceptance within the UN and yet from 1949 through the present Chinese foreign policy has often portrayed China as 'peace-loving' and for the most part it focused on getting China into the UN.

Finally, how did this nationalism develop once containment was successfully dismantled in the expanding circles of recognition? Where did the Chinese leaders find the wisdom to adopt the open door? What was the actual content of the 'open door' policy? What was to be the role of the outside world in China's development? Did new Chinese nationalism bear a grudge against the US? In light of difficulties of containment and UN exclusion how is it that China has become such an ardent supporter of the United Nations? Did the way in which China re-fashioned its fit with the world have anything to do with China's later adaptation to a post-Cold War context of globalization?

Underlying the contemporary rhetoric of peace and idealism is a rationality born of China's own experience. While this rationality is distinguished as Chinese, it is not represented as uniquely Chinese. The contemporary emphasis on ancient Chinese civilization is not for the purposes of fostering competitive robust Chinese nationalism that will forcefully assert China's position in the world as either a 'superpower', or a 'hegemon'. Instead contemporary foreign policy emphasizes that China promotes world peace with its own development. And ancient Chinese civilization is now seen as one of several interacting civilizations, and it is viewed with less inhibition than during the Mao years.

As briefly discussed in Chapter 1, Confucian universalism was unique in its key paternalistic assumption that there could only be one 'Son of Heaven' who would serve as the conduit for the morality immanent in the universe to flow into the human community. The past imperial system formally assumed that 'all men are brothers' particularly as there is latent potential good in all of humanity, but this potential for moral development required adaptation to Chinese moral example in particular.

Chinese civilization is currently one of several. It makes a deliberate contribution to the positive international discourse on the human condition. The Chinese notion of 'diversity of civilization' has challenged Huntington's 'clash of civilizations' with an emphasis on 'tolerance' and open dialogue between civilizations. These developments are analytically interesting; and they need better understanding with reference to the post-1949 history of China's foreign policy and diplomacy.

In his lectures on the 'Three People's Principles' (nationalism, democracy and people's livelihood), Sun Yatsen had inveighed against 'imperialism's' deceptive use of 'cosmopolitanism'. Premier

Zhou Enlai, in the early 1950s, was similarly concerned about US imperialism that he also labelled as '*shijiezhuyi*'. Zhou had criticized Chiang Kai-shek's excessive reliance on the Americans. He rejected American leadership of the free world and he worked on the idea of 'peaceful coexistence' in response to such opportune globalism. He also sought to reinforce China's 'independence and self-reliance' by keeping the lines of communication open with as many peoples and states as possible. China wanted relations with other states but only on the formal basis of reciprocity and equality, and such relations were not to be limited by differences of social system and ideology. Zhou indicated:

> ...we oppose globalism [*shijiezhuyi*], which makes people lose national confidence and seek protection from big powers. The United States advocates globalism and leadership by the big powers in the hope of persuading small countries to follow them forever and of keeping them subjugated and exploited. Our internationalism means the independence and equality of all countries.[1]

'Cleaning Up the House Before Entertaining the Guests'

In the early 1950s response to containment, the Chinese leaders adopted a diplomacy that was designed to crack the walls of containment and to widen China's circle of inter-state relationships on the basis of reciprocity and equality. This policy orientation was characterized as 'cleaning up the house before entertaining the guests'.[2] With state governments they would negotiate on 'the basis of equality, mutual benefit and mutual respect for territorial integrity and sovereignty'.

In this recognition policy one finds the origins of the five principles of peaceful coexistence (*heping gongchu wuxiang yuanze*) that were subsequently highlighted in the 1954 Sino-Indian Agreement on Tibet. These five undertakings, to further mutual benefit and equality, to desist from intervention in the affairs of other states, and to support the principles of non-aggression and peaceful coexistence, subsequently served as the basis for the Chinese negotiating position at Geneva in 1954.

These same principles gave the Chinese a tremendous diplomatic victory over the US at Bandung in 1955.

The fifth principle, 'peaceful coexistence', acquired the key connotation of reserving ideological differences and avoiding military conflict based upon military alliances and the balance of power. This connotation then varied considerably from the first Leninist usage of 'peaceful coexistence' in the early 1920s when 'peaceful coexistence' came up in the course of the transition from 'war communism' to the New Economic Plan and was a tactical breathing space that was needed in preparation for inevitable and final confrontation between different social and ideological systems. The Soviets, for example, signed the Treaty of Rapollo with the Germans on 16 April 1922 so as to counter the balance of power tactics of France's *cordon sanitaire*.

US containment tested New China's diplomacy. China 'resolutely' sided with the Soviet-led socialist world that espoused peace instead of war, but this 'leaning to one side' (*yibian dao*) was a matter of 'leaning'; it did not lead to the full fashioning of an East Asian regional alliance against the US and its allies. Even when China became involved massively in a war with the US on the Korean peninsula, Chinese policy took care not to make a declaration of war so as to preempt the spread of the conflict elsewhere in the region. This was under very trying circumstances as the US crossing of the 38th parallel was assumed to be part of a wider strategy to cross China's northeastern border so as to reverse the course of national liberation. Premier Zhou Enlai claimed that US imperialism 'tried to spread its fires of aggression from Korea to the Chinese mainland in a futile attempt to strangle new-born China by force of arms'.[3]

The UN's door was slammed shut in the face of the Chinese who had just been through a harrowing and complex struggle for national self-determination that had seen US mediation and involvement in China's civil war. 'New China' had every reason to repudiate the UN as a creature of the US majority in the General Assembly. A Chinese delegation told the UN Security Council, on 28 November 1950:

Indeed, without the participation of the lawful delegates of the PRC, representing 475 million people, the United Nations cannot in practice be worthy of its name. Without the participation of the lawful delegates of the People's Republic of China, the Chinese people have no reason to recognize any resolutions or decisions of the United Nations.[4]

On leaving the US on 19 December 1950, this delegation tried to acquire the moral high ground and showed friendly determination in the face of disappointment: 'Although our peace proposal for the suppression of the war [in Korea] was rejected by the Anglo-American ruling bloc without due consideration, yet we are not in despair. We shall continue to strive for peace.'[5]

The claim to support peace was reiterated in the Chinese delegation's stopover in London where it told the British press on 20 December 1950: 'The Chinese people enthusiastically love peace and ardently hope to be able to build their own country peacefully without being subjected to aggression or threat of aggression. The Chinese Government has always advocated the settlement of the existing important questions of the world by peaceful means....'[6]

The Korean War immeasurably complicated the quest for peace, and made recognition all the more difficult and still Chinese policy formally remained open-ended. Premier Zhou spoke to the new diplomatic corps on the dialectics that inform China's approach to world affairs. The corps had a job to do, namely, to expand China's circle of relations. China, he said, would unite with the people of all countries and not just with the people of 'fraternal countries' (i.e., the socialist states). The possibilities for more friendly relations were mixed. Some states were contemplating permanent relations, others were at least 'temporarily friendly'. Drawing from his vast experience in domestic united front negotiations that had involved the US, Zhou claimed:

The capitalist countries by no means form a monolithic bloc, and you should make distinctions among them.... We should be flexible in our diplomatic work, relying on the progressives, uniting with the middle-of-the-road forces and splitting the diehards. In this way we will open up new prospects for diplomatic work. It is wrong to think that the world is divided into conflicting camps and that there is nothing we can do to improve it.[7]

Furthermore, he offered advice in terms that have inspired the low posture in Chinese foreign policy ever since. Zhou said that we must 'mean what we say', while keeping in mind 'it is better not to say too much'. Particularly important was his view that it is better 'to gain the initiative by striking last'. In other words let the other side suffer politically for 'striking first'.

In the past Chiang Kai-shek had to be made responsible for the coming of civil war, and now any tendency to war in the Asia Pacific would be made an American responsibility. At the Foreign Ministry, in June 1953, Zhou specifically instructed that China's identification with peace must be contrasted against the darkly belligerent nature of US policy. Rather than trying to create an alternative 'Asian' alliance against the US, Zhou seized the moral high ground hoping to convince world opinion that 'we are the ones who advocate to resolve all international disputes through peaceful consultation and negotiation, and the other side is the one who insists on the use of force or hostility in resolving conflicts'.[8]

From the early to mid 1950s Chinese foreign policy highlighted the principles of 'independence and self-reliance' as the foundation of New China's diplomacy. Even in the profoundly antagonistic Cold War setting of containment and mutually exclusive ideologies, Zhou and Mao worked on a policy of 'peaceful coexistence' that addressed the gritty differences originating in nationalism, colonial revolution and the ideological conflict between capitalism and socialism.

With the denial of New China's legitimacy and diplomatic credentials at the UN and with constant US pressure to construct anti-China alliances in the Asia Pacific, Chinese diplomatic strategy created a range of formats to encourage friendly relations across the Cold War divide. These developing formats included broadly conceived and interacting formats of state governments, peoples and political parties. Zhou claimed that despite containment China had 'friends the world over'.[9] Neither Zhou nor Mao liked 'neutrality', but they did see the need for flexibility in China's diplomatic strategy for wider recognition. In his September 1951 discussion on the question of 'attitude', Zhou said: 'Generally speaking, there is no such thing as a neutral attitude, but it is possible for a person to waver or to have doubts for a time. We should allow people to take a wait-and-see attitude towards a new phenomenon and even to be skeptical. To express some doubts about a thing doesn't mean you oppose it.'[10]

Establishing the Foundations of Contemporary Foreign Policy at Bandung

Ultimately, Chinese 'peaceful coexistence' placed the emphasis on the importance of national self-determination in Asia as the first principle of all foreign policy analysis. Much of contemporary policy that now deals, for example, with the development of the Shanghai Cooperation Organization, the New Security Concept and the foreign policy of 'harmonious development' can trace its origins back to the application of the five principles of peaceful coexistence at the First Afro-Asian Conference in Bandung in 1955.

Zhou moved decisively to take the high moral ground at Bandung:

> If nations promise not to commit aggression against each other, the way will be paved in international relations for peaceful coexistence. If nations promise not to interfere in each other's internal affairs, it will then be possible for the people of each country to choose their own political system and way of life.[11]

His proposed model of international relations was grounded in his earlier Geneva Conference approach to the Indochina question requiring that countries 'not join any military alliance and that no foreign military bases shall be established on their territory'.

The principles of non-intervention and non-interference were operationalized to discredit US containment. At Bandung, Zhou stated flatly that China would not be exporting revolution to its neighbours. He insisted that China's own successful revolution was generated from within and that any revolution, as a rule, cannot be successfully launched from the outside. Zhou announced that while China was itself the victim of US subversive activities, 'China has no intention whatsoever of subverting the governments of neighbouring countries.'[12] His modus operandi for handling Cold War differences and alignments was to 'seek common ground while reserving differences' (*qiu tong cunyi*). Zhou rejected the export of ideology in favour of common aspirations to development.

Despite the contemporary rigidity of Cold War alignments, Premier Zhou Enlai had the foresight to envisage the day when China's economic development would be supported in a free participation in an international division of labour that would transcend different ideological systems. Under the five principles of peaceful coexistence there was the hope to replace alliances with collective peace (*jiti heping*) and common development.[13] Zhou argued that the US plan to expand regional alliances would exacerbate the differences between Asians. He claimed that the US alliance strategy was deliberately designed to encourage 'Asians to fight Asians'. Summing up, Zhou noted:

> It is the view of the government of the People's Republic of China: Asian countries must *mutually respect each other's independence and sovereignty and not interfere in each other's internal affairs*; they must solve their disputes through peaceful negotiation and not through threats and military force; they must establish normal economic and cultural relations on the basis of *equality and mutual benefit* and disallow discrimination and limitations. Only in this way can the Asian countries avoid the neocolonialist exploitation of the unprecedented catastrophe of Asians fighting Asians and achieve peace and security.[14]

Zhou's five principles model offered a practical approach to post-colonial realities in Asia and immediately responded to the aspirations of the new states in the region. His success was recorded in the articulation of the ten principles of the Bandung Conference that incorporated the entire substance of China's five principles.

US Secretary of State Dulles justified treaties of alliance as necessary against the slippery notions of 'neutralism'. US policy attributed primal significance to alliance making. For the US the extension of pro-Western alliances in the regions of the world was necessary to the protection of the free world. Dulles thus inveighed against the moral bankruptcy of neutrality as a preferred option to participation in military alliances:

> ...these treaties (such as US and ROC treaty) abolish, as between the parties, the principle of neutrality, which pretends that a nation can best gain safety for itself by being indifferent to the fate of others.... The free world today is stronger, and peace is more secure, because so many free nations courageously recognize the now demonstrated fact that their own peace and safety would be endangered by an assault on freedom elsewhere.[15]

The Chinese had neither the inclination nor the resources to play the great power game with Dulles. They had their own approach that was premised in alternative strategy and based upon self-knowledge of their own limited power and resources. The Chinese had just been through a great struggle to achieve national unity; they knew the importance of new nationalism and its need to avoid compromising entangling relations with great powers. Dulles claimed that alliances wonderfully exposed the immorality of neutralism. The Chinese, however, believed that alliances were structurally biased in favour of the great powers at the expense of the principle of equal enjoyment of national self-determination. Great power responsibility had proven itself unable to comprehend the significance of sovereign equality. This assumption formed the basis of the lasting Chinese viewpoint on the bankruptcy of American 'realism'.

The same assumptions lie at the heart of the Sino-Indian fashioning of the five principles of peaceful coexistence. India had been among the first cohort of countries to recognize the PRC, and the Tibetan issue which was a very significant border issue was not allowed to stand in the way as the two countries reserved their differences 'to seek common ground'. Zhou waxed rhetorical on such a fine example of cooperation between 'two ancient and at the same time young countries who eschewed war and were equally devoted to national independence and a peaceful international environment'. Zhou noted Nehru's parliamentary statement that 'the whole approach to the Manila treaty [SEATO] is not only wrong but dangerous' and was grateful for Nehru's support at the Geneva Conference.[16] At Bandung, Nehru had captured the sentiment of new states that resented a forced choice between East and West. Nehru pointedly referred to the 'intolerable humiliation for any nation of Asia or Africa to degrade itself by becoming a camp follower of one or the other of the power blocs'.[17]

The Chinese performance at Bandung is critical to understanding contemporary Chinese foreign policy. At Bandung, Zhou, ever the presumptive Confucian gentleman, acknowledged that indeed there were serious ideological differences between states, but that states could, nevertheless, forthrightly acknowledge such differences and move on to promote common understanding and developmental aspirations.

The Chinese Learning Dialectic

Zhou started to craft a significant policy relation between peace and development that has remained at the centre of Chinese foreign policy statement up to the present. Zhou calculated that inclusive diplomacy and ever widening recognition would contribute to China's development by allowing for the 'learning of the strong points of *all* countries' regardless of whether such countries were 'capitalist' or 'socialist'. Zhou faulted Cold War bourgeois ideology for failing to achieve this kind of intelligent approach. Such ideology confused 'right from wrong' whereas China had tried to 'seek the truth from the facts'.[18] Zhou's response to containment was deliberately inclusive. The five principles offered an alternative guarantee for peace and development in Asia as opposed to war and the inequalities, interference and humiliating second-class status associated with balance of power realism.

At Bandung, Zhou parried the thrust of US diplomacy arguing: 'Though there are many different views among us, and that should not affect the aspirations we all have in common.'[19] The Asian and African states regardless of their constitutional and ideological preferences did have a palpable interest in national economic development, and Cold War politics had only served to fan the flames of 'mutual suspicion and mutual exclusion'. Each country's ideology deserved respect, but it was not to be exported. 'Common aspirations' then coexist with the 'different viewpoints' that together constitute 'an objective reality'.[20]

The direct acknowledgement and reservation of differences now informs the contemporary subscription to 'harmony without uniformity' (*he er butong*). Also in 1955, Premier Zhou laid the original foundation for the present-day 'good neighbourly policy' when he stated: 'On the basis of adherence to the five principles, we are now prepared to establish normal relations with all the Asian and African countries, indeed with all the countries in the world, starting with our neighbours.'[21]

And finally the contemporary foreign policy approach to the 'diversity of civilizations' also has its origins in Zhou's Bandung 'seeking common ground while reserving differences'. In 1955 the 'differences' definitely included religion. Zhou argued: 'Religious freedom is a principle recognized by all modern nations. We Communists are atheists, but we respect all those who have religious beliefs. The days of practicing religious strife should be over because those who profit from such strife are not among us.'[22]

Fitting the PRC into the world was the subject of a key CCP debate in 1956. The debate focused on 'learning' through the deliberate dialectical understanding of domestic and foreign realities. These realities were regarded as in constant flux as they were part of an unfolding universe of hard-to-grasp contradictions. Mao, for example, used his understanding of contradictions to assess the relevance of the Soviet model to China's national economic development as well as a strategy for fitting China into the world that would allow for increased use of foreign technology and knowledge in China's own development. At bottom the prospects for Chinese development were a matter of learning and the 1956 debate about learning later significantly informed the development of Deng Xiaoping's post-1978 'open door' strategy.

Mao Zedong and Zhou Enlai also agreed that it was very important to approach learning with deliberate modesty. Mao no doubt had his moments of ideological grandiloquence when in urging on his comrades he would speak of the future collapse of the capitalist world, but when it came to learning he was known for his aphorisms, *huodao lao, xuedao lao* ('study and live until the day that you die') and *xuexi, xuexi, zai xuexi* ('study, study and study some more'). Mao was, himself, often immodest, but when it came to learning, he professed a politic modesty in the complex dialectical analysis of 'objective' reality. Referring to political celebrations of himself, as the Great Commander, Great Teacher and Great Helmsman, Mao told Edgar Snow in 1970 that it was all a 'nuisance' that would sooner or later be eliminated, but he preferred to be remembered as a primary school teacher.[23]

On commenting on the drafting of the 1954 State Constitution Mao readily recognized the depth of China's underdevelopment; and he asked:

> What can we make at present? ...we can't make a single motor car, plane, tank or tractor. So we mustn't brag and be cocky. Of course I don't mean that we become cocky when we turn out our first car, more cocky when we make 10 cars. And still more cocky when we make more and more cars. That won't do. Even after 50 years when our country is in good shape, we should remain as modest as we are now. If by then we should become conceited and look down on others, it would be bad. We mustn't be conceited even a hundred years from now. We must never be cocky.[24]

On the other hand Mao aggressively outed the brain-dead 'dogmatists' in his own Party who copied the Soviets in everything. Most importantly, Mao believed that critical thought and learning was not confined to socialist states. The Chinese approach to the 'two camps' was based on critical independent study that could be applied to contradictions anywhere. Chinese foreign policy thinking, as it emphasized national independence and self-reliant national economic development, transcended the limits of 'proletarian internationalism'.

The relationship with the Soviets had not proven to be very satisfactory. 'Leaning to one side' (*yibian dao*) was never intended as an absolute arrangement. The Chinese and Soviet leaderships were quite different, as were their respective revolutions. Stalin considered Mao a junior bit-player; and Mao believed that CCP members had paid in blood for Stalin's mistakes during the revolution, and then upon victory, Stalin disputed the legitimacy of the Chinese 'revolution'. Mao believed that China had acquired its own valuable experience and that it was necessary to study deliberately the comparative strengths and weakness of Chinese and Soviet experience. Mao respected the October Revolution, but he was not going to copy automatically the Soviet example. Mao had, for example, already taken significant exception to the Soviet line of 'mechanization before collectivization'. He told his Party that the Soviets had actually made 'mistakes of principle' (*yuancexing cuowu*) in their exclusive and non-dialectical focus on heavy industry.

To those in his own Party who 'slavishly copied' the Soviets, Mao said: 'It is very necessary to win Soviet aid, but the most important thing is self-reliance.' Mao was not refusing foreign aid in general or Soviet foreign aid in particular, but he believed that foreign aid works best in the context of self-reliance and national independence rather than abject and uncritical subservience to the national experience of others. Mao also issued different instructions on this issue. Internally, with regard to Soviet experience and example, he supported the stiffer notion, 'study critically'. In public, he endorsed 'study the advanced experience of the Soviet Union analytically and selectively'.[25]

The inherent flexibility in Chinese 'learning' was also explicit in a 1956 Party conference over the direction of foreign policy. Zhou Enlai identified and criticized two equally mistaken views, 'the parasitic view' and 'the isolationist view'. Zhou rejected reliance on, or the wholesale copying of the Soviet Union. Soviet aid had come at a very high price and it had to be pried from the Soviets' hands. At any rate it was ridiculous to think that the Soviets had both the inclination and the resources ready to shoulder the entire burden of Chinese economic development. The Chinese would largely have to do it on their own, but with a little help from their friends.

The 'isolationists', on the other hand, were blindly overconfident that China would do everything on its own. Autarchy was plainly inconsistent with the assumptions of Chinese Marxism-Leninism, and Zhou contended that achievement of modern national economic development was not possible without participation in the international division of labour.

Despite the rigours of containment Premier Zhou could foresee China taking its rightful place in international exchange on an appropriate basis of national independence and self-reliance; and he refused to focus exclusively on economic relations within the same social and ideological camp. On 16 September 1956 he commented prophetically on China's economic future:

> Facts show not only that economic and technological cooperation among the socialist countries will constantly expand, but also that – as the forces of the peoples of various countries grow daily, the international situation tends and moves towards détente – economic, technological and cultural relations between China and non-socialist countries will expand steadily as well. Therefore, the isolation view…is wrong.[26]

Mao formally set out the dialectical parameters of learning in his famous speech of 25 April 1956, 'On the Ten Major Relationships'. Mao deliberately used ten sets of key political and socio-economic contradictions to advance the Party's critical study of the relative success and failure of the Soviet and Chinese revolutionary experiences. He purposefully set out to ensure that China would not repeat the same mistakes as the Soviet Union. In July 1959 he asked if the Soviets decide to grow pigs in Moslem areas, should Chinese comrades do the same.[27]

On the key point of development strategy as it concerned the dialectical balancing of heavy industry with agriculture and light industry, Mao claimed: '…we have not made *mistakes of principle*. We have done better than the Soviet Union and some Eastern European countries. …[The Soviet] lop-sided stress on heavy industry to the neglect of agriculture and light industry results in a shortage of goods on the market and an unsustainable currency.'[28]

Mao's view of learning required an honest self-knowledge and an intelligent modesty to be applied against subjective 'theatrical pretensions' that come with public ideological statements regarding the superiority of 'socialism'. Alternatively, Mao stressed that 'every nation has its strong points':

> We have put forward the slogan of learning from other countries. I think we have been right. At present, the leaders of some countries are chary... of advancing this slogan. It takes courage to do so, because theatrical pretensions have to be discarded. It must be admitted that every nation has its strong points. If not how can it survive? How can progress be made? On the other hand, every nation has its weak points. Some believe that socialism is just perfect without a single flaw. How can that be true?.... Our policy is to learn from the strong points of all nations and all countries, learn all that is genuinely good in the political, economic, scientific and technological fields and in literature and art.[29]

In all fields of endeavour, including politics and culture as well as science and technology, Mao urged the Party to look beyond its own propaganda and to extend the process of learning beyond the borders of the socialist camp.

In 'On the Ten Major Relationships' Mao moved away beyond the thinking of his mentor, Li Dazhao. Mao stresssed the importance of modesty even as he considered the latent potential for development that comes with China's status as 'poor and blank': 'Being poor and blank is therefore all to our good. Even when one day our country becomes strong and prosperous, we must still adhere to the revolutionary stand, *remain modest and prudent*, learn from other countries and not allow ourselves to become swollen with conceit.'[30]

In his 'A Talk to the Music Workers' on 24 August 1956, Mao further clarified the parameters of learning: 'We must oppose dogmatism and conservatism. Neither will do China any good. Studying things foreign isn't equivalent to copying them all. We learn from the ancients to benefit the living, and we learn from foreigners to benefit the Chinese people.' Mao elaborated: 'By absorbing the good points of foreign countries, we will be able to make our own things leap ahead. *The Chinese and the foreign should be combined and become an organic whole and there shouldn't be indiscriminate use of foreign things.*'[31]

Resolving the Outstanding Contradiction within Foreign Policy

There is an impressive policy continuity that informed the first years of 'cleaning up the house before entertaining the guests' and was then carried forward into the next and arguably most important stage of policy development culminating in the application of the five principles and their corollary, 'seek common ground and reserve differences' at Bandung. Such strategy was well designed to facilitate the modest learning of the 'strong points of all nations' as it promoted an ever widening progress of recognition across the Cold War divide. This ascending trend, however, had to contend with the unresolved contradiction that lies at the heart of 'proletarian internationalism'.

For the *classicus locus* of the latter term one has to go at least as far back as Lenin's 1920 Report to the Second Comintern Congress. The cause of socialism had floundered in Europe, but there was the hope that the international progress of socialism could draw on victory in one country, the Soviet Union. Proletarian internationalism required an active political stance, placing the interests of the world-wide proletarian struggle above those of national struggle. Lenin warned of the need to guard against 'deep-rooted petty-bourgeois national prejudices'. According to Lenin's prescription, 'proletarian internationalism'

> ...demands first, that the interests of the proletarian struggle in any one country should be subordinated to the interests of that struggle on a world-wide scale, and second, that a nation which is achieving victory over the bourgeoisie should be able and willing to make the greatest national sacrifices for the overthrow of international capital.[32]

In short, this view supported the export of revolution and active involvement to support anti-government forces in the colonial and neo-colonial context. Such development conflicted with the five principles of peaceful coexistence in that the latter clearly emphasized the supreme importance of national self-determination and the importance of non-interference in the political affairs of other states.

At Bandung Zhou may have been more concerned about Asia than East Europe. At any rate, he did not have to deal with 'proletarian internationalism'. The issue of peaceful coexistence came to a head in the mid 1960s with new international focus on 'national liberation'. The latter issue complicated progress from the original Bandung Conference towards a Second Afro-Asian Conference in 1965. At a press conference in Cairo, 20 December 1963, Zhou claimed that 'one of the main contents' of Chinese foreign policy concerns 'active support for the national democratic movements in Asia, Africa and Latin America'. The 'obligation of support', however, was interpreted in terms of new national movements largely relying on 'their own strength'.[33] Subsequently, Zhou indicated in a speech in Algeria on Christmas Day, 1953: 'The truth of revolutions cannot be monopolized. The revolutionaries of all countries will find the way for revolution suitable to the realities of their own country....'[34]

Chinese diplomacy was conflicted over the need to give greater support to national liberation, and in the developing ideological dispute with the Soviet Union the Chinese complained of how Khrushchev was using 'peaceful coexistence' with the US to undermine national liberation in the Third World. The problem was explicit in Sukarno's advice to Zhou Enlai: '...there can be no talk of peaceful coexistence with imperialism'.[35]

The Chinese wanted wider recognition. They wished 'to support' wars of national liberation against US imperialism, but how could they achieve this without compromising the substance of the five principles? Wherever he went in the Third World, Premier Zhou talked up the five principles of peaceful coexistence and the ten Bandung principles. He indicated that people wanted revolution, but he also indicated that revolution was essentially a matter of 'self-reliance', and that this did not preclude foreign aid and economic cooperation between friendly states. Moreover, Zhou again attempted to put the onus for war on the US: 'The Five Principles of Peaceful Coexistence put forward by China can all be found in the United Nations Charter, but the United States rejected them. So you can see who violates the United Nations Charter.'[36]

Essentially, the consensus that animated the smaller forum of Asian and African states that had met in Bandung in 1955 was not easy to revive in the face of the early to mid 1960s cleavages over fast-spreading national liberation in Africa. Moreover, the attempt to create a second Bandung at Algiers was complicated not only by the crucial rift between the Chinese and Indians over their borders, but also by the deepening Sino-Soviet split and the potentially alternative focus on the non-aligned movement. Despite Chinese efforts to make 'good preparations' for the Second Afro-Asian Conference based on 'two methods', namely, 'seeking common ground while reserving differences' and letting the 'Asian and African countries settle their own problems, without intervention by imperialism', the bid to repeat the Bandung experience failed.[37]

The Chinese politically encouraged national liberation around the world so as to weaken US domination of world politics. This got in the way of USSR progression towards an understanding that would later lead to détente with the US. Mao insisted that Soviets exercise needed leadership. He was not suggesting that China take the lead, but he held the Soviet feet to the fire on the issue of 'peaceful transition' where Nikita Khrushchev had argued that there was in the new era less need to think in terms of revolution as a violent act dissolving the existing state, and a pressing need to consider the possibilities of social democratic parties winning at the ballot box obviating the need for the proletarian 'smashing of the state'.

The Russians were not about to allow Chinese enthusiasm for revolution and national liberation undermine their far more important relationship with the US. The Chinese in turn increasingly had to conclude that the Sino-Soviet Treaty of Mutual Friendship was a very thin reed of socialist fraternity.

The Soviets had already given them several hard lessons in the importance of 'self-reliance'. There was the prime example of the Sino-Indian border war of 1962, when the Soviets broke ranks with their fraternal cousins in Beijing and disregarded the basic requirements of 'proletarian internationalism'. The Soviets focused their energies on Camp David Talks, closing their ears to Chinese entreaties for international support during the border clash. The *People's Daily* was outraged: 'Here is the first instance in history in which a related socialist country, instead of condemning the armed provocations of the reactionaries of a capitalist country, condemned another fraternal socialist country when it was confronted with such armed provocation.'[38] The obvious deterioration in Sino-Soviet relations reinforced the Chinese in their commitment to national independence and self-reliance, but what of the outstanding tension between peaceful coexistence and proletarian internationalism?

Foreign Policy and the Cultural Revolution

'Proletarian internationalism' did not survive the wild gyrations of the Cultural Revolution. Red Guard extremism briefly targeted the notion of peaceful coexistence. In the uncontrolled contest of class struggle, almost the entire diplomatic corps was recalled; the Foreign Ministry was actually taken over in a 'power seizure'; Chen Yi, the Foreign Minister, was subjected to Red Guard criticism for supporting the UN and ignoring national liberation, and Chinese leftists created unauthorized incidents in Burma, Cambodia, Nepal and Ceylon.[39] Zhou called on the left to eschew violence and to struggle 'showing facts and reasoning'. An occupation of the Soviet embassy was barely avoided.[40] The propagation of Mao's thought led to widespread riots in Hong Kong. Zhou's promise at Bandung not to become involved in local politics seemed irrelevant. This 'leftist' phase culminated in the burning of the British embassy. Essentially the underlying rationality and success of the five principles gained attention in light of such excesses. Mao, believing that China's reputation was suffering irreparable harm abroad, moved to support Zhou Enlai who regained control of the Foreign Ministry. And in the last phase of the Cultural Revolution Mao and Zhou worked on normalization with the US on the basis of the re-stated five principles of peaceful coexistence.

Even in the 'leftist phase' of the mid 1960s the underlying rationality of foreign policy was not completely subsumed. The extent of China's reach was minimal in material terms, but greater in the political terms of shrill propaganda and rhetoric. Chinese policy response to the world was to identify complexity and to keep as many options open as possible, avoiding absolutes and direct military involvement in other countries. It is important to note the rather modest support the Chinese offered for national liberation.

Albert Feuerwerker provided the following insight as to the limits of Chinese engagement as it is governed by a 'strong reality factor' in China's post-1949 foreign policy:

> First, support of wars of national liberation by the PRC – in the form of clandestine arms shipments and military training, but more importantly and more commonly by favorable propaganda and political relations with revolutionary organizations – has in fact been more a product of the short-range tactical needs of the Chinese nation-state than of any ultimate Maoist program.... In 1963, for example, China endorsed 23 out of a possible 120 revolutionary armed struggles in Asia, Latin America and Africa. And the pattern of endorsement which mostly took the form of propaganda support, identifies this policy as the tactic of a relatively weak state attempting to keep the United States off balance and to coerce support from other Third World states for China's aspirations, for a larger and recognized role in the international system.[41]

What then of Lin Biao's famous tract on the victory of the people's war? There was a necessary economy in political as opposed to genuine military solutions. The objective was not to destroy the US homeland *per se*, but to keep the US off its game by challenging the underlying weakness of US imperialism overseas and politically encouraging the spread of national liberation at the expense of US hegemony.

Lin Biao's 'Long Live the Victory of the People's War' included a scary rhetoric whereby the developed countries would be encircled by the developing countryside. The essay also reiterated Mao's axiom, 'We must despise the enemy strategically and take full account of him tactically.'[42] The latter required prudent adaptation to the superiority of the US military while 'people's war' was essentially predicated in the making of self-reliant revolution on one's own soil. This was a key aspect of the 'propaganda' highlighted in Feuerwerker's analysis, and, indeed, such propaganda was seldom backed up by sustained Chinese military force outside China's own borders. Even in its brief 'revolutarionary' phase during the mid 1960s, Chinese foreign policy lacked a significant irredentist component.

Against the background of Nixon's journey for peace, a September 1971 Gallup poll reported that more than 50 per cent of Americans surveyed believed that China is the greatest threat to world peace. Allen Whiting, a leading academic and former Director of Far Eastern intelligence analysis at the US Department of State, noted the findings of his study of the nine cases where the People's Liberation Army (PLA) 'crossed customary borders in hostile array' between 1949 and 1971: '...the government in Peking, in most cases deployed the PLA in defensive reaction against a perceived threat. The Chinese use of force primarily for defensive deterrence has remained remarkably consistent....'[43]

The runaway dynamics of Red Guard politics in the Cultural Revolution led to embarrassing dysfunction. 'Leftist adventurism' had grossly over-extended itself and was short-lived. Even within the context of the Cultural Revolution, a new breakthrough occurred in policy. Zhou Enlai and Mao met with Henry Kissinger to organize Sino-US normalization in 1971.

Plumbing the Depths of Chinese Foreign Policy 'Pragmatism'

The five principles of peaceful coexistence emerged out of the chaos of the Cultural Revolution to provide the basis for completing the recognition process that undermined the US containment of China. The predication of Sino-US normalization upon these principles was particularly important, but how did this actually happen? Were the Chinese leaders suddenly rational where once they had been ideological? The five principles were not used to discredit ideology. In fact they supported normalization on the basis of respect for differences of ideology, rather than the elimination of ideology.

The lessons learned on the importance of national independence and self-reliance, were part of ideology as it emphasized praxis and the dialectical understanding of the contradictions that underlie the realities of the world. This 'pragmatism' had 'Chinese characteristics', and it certainly was not the 'pragmatism' (*shiyongzhuyi*) of John Dewey. Mao distinguished between 'pragmatism' that was praxis synthesized with theory on the basis of 'seeking the truth from the facts' and 'bourgeois pragmatism'.

Mao told Party members to strive for a 'modesty compatible with reality'. They were to apply dialectics so as to unlock the complexity of reality and to fashion a strategy of modernization that would overcome significant material difficulties. Reflecting on how to 'make the high mountain bow its head' and to 'make the river yield the way', Mao stood his ground versus nay-saying doubters in the West, saying: 'No, we are not insane; we are pragmatists [*shjizhuyizhe*]; we are Marxists seeking the truth from the facts.'[44]

Zhou Enlai and Deng Xiaoping used Mao's theory of contradiction in their understanding of the competing realities of international relations and in their strategizing for modernization and development. While foreign policy sought ever-widening circles of recognition on the basis of these principles, the leadership in Beijing was not simply going to join the club of great powers and take out subscriptions to Western journals on realism. The Chinese 'pragmatism' that fostered Sino-US normalization originated in Chinese experience and thinking. In reply to criticism that the united front tactic to win over the middle will result in the strategic loss of revolutionary virtue, Zhou Enlai replied that a genuine socialist policy must achieve the 'dialectical unity of firm principles and great flexibility'.[45] This perspective originated in thinking about the domestic politics of the Chinese revolution and had virtually nothing to do with Henry Kissinger's Western notion of 'pragmatism'.

There was, nevertheless, an early meeting of the minds as to the importance of reserving 'differences', and Kissinger later wrote of how Zhou was his 'first teacher' on Chinese affairs.[46] As an ambitious Harvard professor Kissinger had distinguished between 'charismatic' and 'bureaucratic-pragmatic' leaderships, and he had claimed that although excessive pragmatism might result in a failure to achieve positive direction, in a society consumed by ideological necessity, there is an absolute failure to innovate due to rigid doctrinal exegesis premised in the assumption of absolute 'objectivity'.[47] Kissinger liked the way that Zhou ranged across so many discrete points of analysis while retaining a consistent strategic focus. In Beijing the National Security Advisor and the Harvard Professor came into unwitting conflict. To follow through with Kissinger's logic, one might conclude that Zhou was somehow a coolly rational and unsentimental leader in a revolutionary state which epitomized 'charismatic authority' and touted its own absolute 'objectivity'.

Kissinger disliked ideology. He was not predisposed to looking for the source of Chinese 'pragmatism' in Mao's ideology. President Nixon's own writings cited Kissinger's early view that the Chinese leadership is 'close to fanatic in the intensity of their beliefs'. Kissinger said to Huang Hua after meeting Zhou: 'We thought that you'd bump the table and shout "Down with American Imperialism".' Kissinger was fascinated with Zhou Enlai's mastery of geopolitics, and he wrote: '[Zhou] was a dedicated ideologue, but he used the faith that had sustained him through decades of struggle to discipline a passionate nature into one of the most acute and unsentimental assessments of reality that I have encountered.'[48]

But then ideology apparently counted for something as Kissinger later wrote that the Sino-Soviet conflict was 'primeval'. Putting on his Harvard hat, he warned: 'In systems based on infallible truth there can only be one authorized interpretation: a rival claim to represent true orthodoxy is a moral challenge.'[49]

Although Kissinger regarded Zhou as a fellow practitioner, he acknowledged some difference when it came to relations with the Soviets. As more recent transcripts reveal, Kissinger was somewhat defensive about the softness, or deftness in the US approach to US–Soviet relations. The following exchange of 12 November 1973 is illustrative of duly observed difference:

Secretary Kissinger: I explained to the Prime Minister... our tactics are more complex and maybe less heroic, but our strategy is the same. We have no doubt who is the principal threat to the world today.

Chairman Mao: What you do is a Chinese kind of shadow boxing. (*laughter*) We do a kind of shadow boxing which is more energetic.

Prime Minister Zhou: And direct in its blows.[50]

Kissinger characterized Mao and Zhou as 'scientists of equilibrium', and he presumed: 'China was in the great classical tradition of European statesmanship.'[51]

A reading of Zhou Enlai's *Selected Works* indicates that Zhou believed China's diplomacy was rooted in Mao Zedong ideology, not as dogma, but as a 'scientific explanation' of the contradictions that inform politics and material reality at the entwined domestic and international levels. Zhou Enlai well understood Western 'realism' and 'balance of power' thinking, but this does not mean he, himself, subscribed to Kissinger's balance of power as the basis for China's own diplomacy and related foreign policy. Kissinger's realism treated Chinese ideology as a 'façade' that masked the sophisticated practice of the balance of power.

Deng Xiaoping Places China in the World

Mao's China and Deng's China represented a continuum of changing ideology, rather than a suppression of ideology in modernist pragmatism. Deng Xiaoping's line and policies were developed straight out of 'Mao Zedong Thought' including the key policy regarding China's relation to the world, 'open door' and 'self-reliance'.

Deng, the 'pragmatist', is usually contrasted with Mao, the 'revolutionary'; however, Deng Xiaoping took up where Mao and Zhou Enlai left off. Deng did uproot the ideological extremism of the Cultural Revolution, particularly with respect to 'class struggle as the key link' (*yi jieji douzheng wei gang*), but analysis has often neglected the extent to which Deng developed his new programme of economic reform and open door on the basis of past policy perspective and ideological sanction. Deng built upon a politics

of consensus that claimed deliberate ideological continuity. Zhou
had earlier featured the notion of 'four modernizations', in 1963
and again in 1974.

Deng went to the UN in 1974. He opposed the five principles
of peaceful coexistence to 'hegemony' and distinguished between
'self-reliance' and 'autarchy'. He picked up on Zhou's 1960s view
that self-reliance was a rational matter of national independence
and that it was on such a basis that China or any developing
economy could freely seek foreign aid and economic cooperation
with friendly countries.

In the first speech to the UN by a senior CCP leader, Deng
complained of the 'ideas of pessimism and helplessness spread by
imperialism in connection with the question of the development of
developing countries', and it was in this context that he explained
the key distinction between 'self-reliance' and 'self-seclusion'. He
disagreed with Western criticism that 'self-reliance' was a nativist
irrationality which defied the modern division of labour in the
world economy.

'Self-reliance', as it had been originally used in the CCP's
revolutionary progress, entwined themes of revolution and
socialism and connoted 'standing on one's own to change to
a new life'.[52] Deng clarified: 'By self-reliance we mean that a
country should mainly rely on the strength and wisdom of its own
people, control its own economic lifelines, make full use of its own
resources, strive hard to increase food production, and develop its
national economy step by step and in a planned way.'[53] Deng no
doubt was drawing on a continuous perspective on international
change; however, whereas Zhou had once complained about US
'globalism' in the 1950s, in the mid 1970s China had to assert its
independence in a more complex world of US hegemonism and
Soviet 'socialist imperialism'.

Deng revised Mao on a number of important points. He
dropped Mao's focus on the general trend to world war to focus
on peace and development (*heping yu fazhan*). This required the
reiteration of the five principles of peaceful coexistence. Opposition
to hegemonism did not mean that China could not increase its
trade with the American and Soviet hegemons. Moreover, Deng

provided a definitive view on the Cold War history of Chinese foreign policy and international relations when he indicated in 1984:

> The Five Principles of Peaceful Coexistence provide the best way to handle the relations between nations. Other ways – thinking in terms of 'the socialist community', 'bloc politics' or 'spheres of influence', for example – lead to conflict, heightening international tensions. Looking at the history of international relations, we find that the Five Principles of Peaceful Coexistence have a potentially wide application.[54]

Deng subsequently summed up the content of China's 'independent foreign policy' as follows: 'We adhere to an independent foreign policy of peace and do not join any bloc. We are prepared to maintain contacts and make friends with everyone. We are against any country that practices hegemonism. We are against any country that commits aggression against others. We are clear in our words and in our deeds.'[55]

Deng disassociated Mao from the Gang of Four. The latter were criminals. Mao, however misguided in his last years, had founded the People's Republic of China on the basis of Mao Zedong Thought; and the latter was essentially the collective wisdom of a revolutionary generation that inspired Party rule. While acknowledging that Mao had made 'comprehensive errors', Deng launched reform on the 1956 basis of Mao's 'On the Ten Major Relationships' and Mao's speech to the music workers.

These documents were widely circulated to foster Mao's learning dialectic. Modernization required 'liberation of the mind' and experimentation with new ways of doing things in the economy just as was the case in the border region struggles of 1940 when the CCP faced the Japanese imperial army and the Guomindang's blockade. Deng's new special economic zones were the contemporary counterparts of the 1940s border region governments.

In a media report of his discussion with Guangdong Party leaders, for example, he had freely speculated on the contemporary relevance of revolutionary history:

They started their conversation with Yanan, touching on how such a tiny border area in those years [early 1940s] managed to capture the whole country. When talking about how people in the old revolutionary base areas and frontier area were still not affluent after several decades of liberation, all sorts of feeling came to their minds.[56]

On many occasions, Zhou Enlai had cued Deng on how to proceed with the 'four modernizations' based on 'seeking the truth from the facts'. After Zhou's death, Deng essentially summed up:

To seek the truth from the facts, we must proceed from reality in all things. New problems and new solutions in domestic and foreign affairs were to be deliberately predicated in integrating theory with practice and 'proceeding from reality in all things' [yi qie cong shiji chufa].[57]

When asked by US broadcaster Mike Wallace what he thought Mao's reaction might be to China today, Deng simply replied: 'There are differences. However, there are similarities as far as certain principles are concerned. Mao Zedong Thought is still our guiding ideology.'[58] Deng may have taken Mao Zedong Thought well beyond what Mao himself would have found acceptable, but Mao Zedong Thought provided the only vehicle by which to further continue Party rule and modernization at the same time.

The progress of Deng's reform was significantly interrupted in the events of 1989 when the suppression in Tiananmen Square was followed by severe international censure and trade sanctions. Deng refused to allow a return to the Cultural Revolutionary focus on class struggle against counterrevolution, but he had to work to ensure against any international tendencies to contain China for its alleged human rights abuses. The collapse of the Soviet Union was cause for introspection and depressed anxiety, but Deng told China's diplomats that they must not worry about unprecedented developments. Deng summed up the international situation in just over three sentences:

First, we should observe the situation coolly. Second, we should hold our ground. Third, we should act calmly. Don't be impatient; it is not good to be impatient. We should be calm, calm and again calm, and quietly immerse ourselves in practical work to accomplish something – something for China.[59]

Drawing on a tradition of patient fortitude and modesty Deng also instructed: 'The more developed we are, the more modest we should be.'[60] He believed that the more China developed, the more this would attract the concern of the developed countries:

China will have tremendous influence. Of course that will put the developed countries all the more on guard against us. Notwithstanding we should maintain friendly exchanges with them. We should hold them as friends, but also have an understanding of what they are doing. We should not criticize or condemn other countries without good reasons or go to extremes in our words and deeds.[61]

When it came time for Deng to hand over the baton of leadership to the next generation his advice reflected what he had learned from Mao and Zhou: Deng had well learned the underlying principles that resulted in their Bandung recognition strategy that had undermined US containment.

Deng Xiaoping's 'new' line on 'peace and development' borrowed significantly from past ideas, perspectives and directives of Mao and Zhou. Mao and Zhou had established several enduring lessons concerning learning to support development. Their open but critical attitude sought to fit China into the world on the basis of a practical rationality that rejected not only 'blind Westernization', but also 'dogmatism'. Their approach was deliberately premised in a modesty that wisely challenged an overly nationalistic approach that supported 'isolationism', or 'Chinese exceptionalism'.

Deng's consensus building was based on Mao's dialectics – a strategy for change based upon deliberate ideological continuity that dealt with differences within unity. Zhou Enlai had shown the way in this. Zhou's adaptation to Mao's dialectics in China's new international relations was based on the strategy, 'seeking common ground while reserving differences'. Zhou had originally explained: 'Unity is formed and grows amid contradiction.... Unity means that parties to a contradiction are united in common ground.

The unity of contradictions does not impede the development of individuality.'[62]

To be sure, there were times when revolutionary rhetoric was used to deter enemies in the outside world, but at the core of the Mao–Zhou–Deng 'pragmatism' is a self-conscious process of dialectical learning that rejects moral absolutes and requires modesty in the face of every changing reality. In the face of great adversity and constant change, this rationality greatly facilitated China's fit with the world.

3

CONNECTING THE 'RULE OF LAW', 'HUMAN RIGHTS' AND 'DEMOCRACY' IN CHINA

As discussed in Chapter 1, Mme Song was optimistic that China could build on its ancient civilization while bringing about a new 'constitutionalism' (*xianzheng*). Some Western critics would otherwise contend that China is committing 'cultural relativism' in its approach to concepts that are universal in nature and that no progress is possible given the hopeless totalitarian nature of the regime, hence the Chinese focus on 'Chinese characteristics' is a political distraction from the real task at hand which is the comprehensive and genuine development of the rule of law, human rights and democracy in China as these terms have been defined in the West.

Even so, Mme Song was not necessarily wrong in her thinking about China's future as characterized by some form of synthesis that would regard a focus on local conditions as legitimate. As we have seen, even Mao Zedong had approached this question about learning and adaptation on the basis of a learning dialectic that would critically distinguish and synthesize Chinese and outside experience. This mindset assumed that China has some of its own 'strong points', but then the capitalist countries also have their strong points. Mao avowed that China ought to learn the latter where appropriate. This raises the question as to what kind of synthesis will pay the best dividend in the development of modern China.

The 'rule of law' (*fazhi*), 'human rights' (*renquan*) and 'democracy' (*minzhuzhuyi*) are key concepts have been extensively imported into China, but there is very little in China's 'ancient civilization' that provides for their quick and easy assimilation within today's political culture and public consciousness. These terms have come into China's modern political vocabulary under the aegis of the Party; and these terms are widely used both in formal policy statements and in public discourse. The following analysis connects the dots between these concepts, placing their use and interrelationship within the domestic political and social context of reform.

'Constitutionalism' (*xianzheng*) is an issue that has received considerable attention in the contemporary development of China's public policy studies. Li Buyun, an authority on 'democracy' and 'human rights' and currently Director of the Public Law Research Centre at the Institute of Law, CASS, notes that while Mao had used 'constitutionalism' against Chiang Kai-shek, after 1949 the term all but disappeared. It was not really resuscitated until the convening of two major conferences in 1992. Li himself defines the term as follows:

> ...constitutionalism [is] a political system which regards the realization of a series of democratic principles and system as its main content, the rule of law as its basic guarantee, and the fulfillment of the most extensive human rights as its goal. Under constitutionalism a country is managed by the constitution which embodies the ideals of modern civilization. Of the three key elements of constitutionalism, democracy is the foundation, rule of law is one of the important conditions, and the guarantee of human rights is the goal.[1]

Li is an influential trendsetter but sometimes he has moved too quickly beyond mainstream Party opinion; however, in the 2005 official White Paper on building political democracy the correlations of these three concepts were pursued in roughly the same manner.

Also Hu Jintao has personally maintained earlier reference to the rule of law and human rights while making increasing current reference to democracy. The latter is defined in the 2005 White Paper as actualizing the will of the 'overwhelming majority of people' and 'protecting their rights and interests'.[2] The same

White Paper called for the integration of party leadership with 'the people's status as the masters of their own affairs, and governance of the country according to the rule of law'.

Party argument assumes that the Party, itself, will guarantee the supremacy of law over all organization including all political parties. This commitment does not appear to fit all that well with the conventions of democratic centralism and flies in the face of Western critics who assume that the Party is part of the problem rather than part of the solution. Still, during the reform years there have been significant changes in the Party's terms of reference. Deng Xiaoping, for example, required the following new understanding on the part of the Party's powerful Central Committee for Discipline Inspection:

> It is not appropriate for the Party to concern itself with matters that fall within the scope of the law. If the Party intervenes in everything, the people will never acquire a sense of the rule of law. The Party should concern itself with inner-Party discipline, leaving problems that fall within the scope the law to the state and government.[3]

Hu Jintao has increasingly emphasized 'democracy' as he has focused on the 'ruling party' (*zhizheng dang*). This 'governing party' claims that it is updating itself and it will do more to embrace the 'people, first' by going beyond establishing the revolution to deal with today's developmental questions in a new complex world that includes inevitable globalization. However, this same 'governing party' continues to subscribe to Deng Xiaoping's March 1979 'four cardinal principles' (*sixiang jiben yuanze*) even while it talks of democratic governance as participation in the public management of public affairs.[4] Western observers are in disagreement as to the possibilities, with Jude Howell, for example, noting that '...the dominance of the Party will continue to constrain progress in governance reforms'.[5]

Under reform the state is no longer a simple unified extension of class struggle and the Party's contemporary focus is now on the management of public affairs.[6] David Ding, in *Democracy Since Tiananmen Square* (2001), for example, discusses the new intellectual viewpoint on 'democracy':

The new scholarly understanding of democracy…marks a qualitative change and a clear break from orthodox Leninism, which it now views as a justification of authoritarianism – understood as the domination of society by an unlimited state power. This new understanding indicates the conceptual differentiation of society from the state, emphasizing societal autonomy, economic freedom, and the recognition of diverse and equal social interests. Democracy is consequently understood as the control of a limited state by an independent society and the accommodation and coordination of diverse social interests in the political process.[7]

Under Hu's focus on the 'governing party', the Party has been asking similar questions about the contemporary relevance of 'democracy'. There is an explicitly stated political awareness that the Party has to respond to 'public feeling' and to protect rights and interests if it is going to survive. How will it respond? Article 2 of the State Administration notes that the 'People will administer State affairs and manage economic and cultural undertakings and social affairs through various channels and in various ways in accordance with the provisions of the law.' However, Article 3 subsequently indicates: 'The state organs of the PRC apply the principle of democratic centralism.'[8]

Essentially, China is still a one-party state and there are still eight democratic parties. CCP analysis continues to argue that China has a cooperative rather than a competitive multi-party system and that there is now closer and regular cooperation between the NPC and the Chinese People's Political Consultative Conference, a traditional united front vehicle for gaining wide-ranging support in various sectors of society for the policies of the day.

The regime adheres to a conception of 'socialist democracy' that focuses on the rights and interests of the people, and it has begun to respond to the notion of 'civil society' (*shimin shehui*). The Party is no longer in the same position of being able to monopolize popular organization. The established national mass organizations no longer have a functional monopoly over activity in their specific spheres of endeavour, such as in the area of women's activity or workers' activity. Now the mass organizations, which are themselves undergoing institutional change, often have to cooperate with secondary organizations; and there has been a related proliferation of so-called NGOs and/or GONGOs (government-organized NGOs).[9] The Party's delegated managers of the functional divisions of Chinese society have now to forge new cooperative arrangements with 'secondary organization' that is semi-autonomous in its resources, personnel and its public and sometimes international support. The language and syntax of contemporary Chinese politics has undergone interesting and even profound change.

Zhou Tianyong, Deputy Director, Research Office of the Party School of the CCPCC, was asked about the new book sensation, *Storming the Fortress*. Specifically, his interviewer asked about the book's claim that China would 'become a democratic country under the rule of law by 2020'.

Zhou responded that there are three levels of meanings:

> First, on the level of the ruling party, the CPC must promote and guarantee law-based administration. Second, the framework of checks and balances between the NPC, the executive and judicial bodies must be realized. ...Third, non-governmental organizations should be thoroughly developed and the people's awareness of democracy and the rule of law substantially improved.[10]

Connecting the 'Rule of Law', 'Human Rights' and 'Democracy'

In December 1978 Deng Xiaoping formally entwined 'democratization and legalization' as a critical part of early reform strategy that sought stability and economic growth through a new institutional strategy that rejected outright the extremes of class struggle and alternatively focused attention on the 'four modernizations' and economic reform and the open door. This led to major political focus on the 'rule of law' versus 'rule of man' in national debates and media coverage of the early to mid 1980s. The issue was palpable for many CCP leaders who had lost their constitutional rights in the power seizures of the Cultural Revolution. New institutionalization including the 'rule of law' was to replace the 'rule of man', or the 'spirit of the leader' so as to ensure China's political stability against any future reoccurrence of cultural revolution and also to provide a predictable basis for modern economic activities.

After several cycles of national debate, the 'rule of law' (*fazhi*) was enshrined in the State Constitution for the first time in March 1999 amendment, stating that China is 'a socialist country under a rule of law' (Article 5 amended). A consistent and striking new constitutional reference to 'human rights' followed in a 2004 amendment that not only confirmed the 'lawful interests of the individual and private sectors of the economy, but for the first time in a revision to Article 33 the Constitution noted: 'The State respects and preserves human rights.' There has been no similar new constitutional amendment on democracy but this is not impossible given the CCPCC decision on Party governance of 2004 and the 2005 White Paper on 'building political democracy' that focused comprehensively on the regime's developing understanding of 'democracy' in China.

Such amendments and political focus formally suggest a guarded but observable sequence of reforms that deliberately and sequentially moved through the contents of the 'rule of law', 'human rights' and 'democracy' rather than moving equally on all three fronts within a predetermined synchronicity. Conceptually, if not practically, these emphases have recently become more interrelated, entwined and mutually supportive. Chinese reform has moved in deliberate increments and on the basis of reserved experiment rather than in a comprehensive all-fronts manner.

The first and second chapters of this book argued that the Cold War assumptions concerning the inward-looking nativist nature of the CCP leadership are not sustained in the historical facts of actual policy and perspective. There was a disposition to learn based upon modesty and the assumption of independence and equality. How then have the Chinese reacted to apparent Western notions of the rule of law, human rights and democracy? These concepts were learned in political context for domestic purposes and they have been deliberately fitted into local conditions and perspective.

The Confucian Past in the Constitutional Present

As suggested in the following brief review of the fundamental assumptions of traditional Confucian governance, the magnitude and complexity of the problem of learning about the three concepts should not be underestimated. In the Chinese tradition the state became an extension of society based upon a deep sense of the need for familial harmony. Power in this context was legitimated in an absolute moral paternalism of the Emperor as the 'Son of Heaven'. The essential purpose of Confucian governance was to provide a moral example to society. The difference between right and wrong was to be outlined in teaching by using one's own moral example, *shenjiao*.

The redeeming feature of this tradition, at least for some Western missionaries, was the idea that the potential for goodness is implicit in all of humankind, but where in the West there was an essential working notion of equality that supported the notion of citizenship, based on a core principle of equality, the Confucian tradition accepted a moral hierarchy that was characterized by inequality. Even Sun Yatsen, when he crafted his 'Three People's Principles', including the principle of democracy, noted that inequality was intrinsic to human society. In Sun's view there was no natural equality among men and human society tended to amplify inequalities. Even when the kings of Europe were brought down and people began to believe in equality, Sun opined: 'They did not know that such a thing is impossible',[11] and that it was important to yield to the talent of those who are morally superior in exercising the 'power of government'.

In the Confucian tradition, those who are morally superior are justified in their rule over those who are morally inferior. There was no need to think about 'constitutionalism'. What need is there for protection against what is moral? Confucianism reinforced the societal distinctions between moral superiority and inferiority with exacting principles of decorum and 'orthopraxy' or formal protocols of speech that served to consolidate the social hierarchy.[12]

In this tradition there was no natural interest or focus on the importance of equality underwriting either a notion of citizenship that stressed the self-realization of the informed citizen in politics, nor was there any need for systems of representation requiring that citizen's interests be aggregated by elected officials to influence the formation of government policy. The Confucian official was not a representative. He was a moral exemplar whose job it was to nurture the morally inferior mass of society.

In the Confucian tradition subjects were supposed to be in absolute awe of the moral example of the Son of Heaven. Political questioning of the Emperor's right to rule became a form of extreme heresy, *danibudao*. There was no need for a 'loyal opposition' and any opposition was in serious danger of being labelled as heresy. Similarly, there was no need to protect the citizen from the state as a moral enterprise. The idea of using law against privilege and power so as to protect each individual as a 'rights bearing individual' would have seemed not only strange but subversive to the ears of Confucian officials. The response of the famous late-nineteenth-century official, Zhang Zhidong, to the advent of assemblies was instructive. Assemblies were talk shops for loud mouths where there was a preponderance of self-serving, profit driven merchants who 'are skilled in trickery' and do not have a natural interest in moral governance.[13]

The past offered the present very little in terms of conceptual equivalence that could be utilized in the fostering of 'constitutionalism'. However, a review of events since the launching of open door and economic reform in December 1978 confirms a key sequence in the Chinese political approach to the related subjects of 'rule of law', 'human rights' and 'democracy'. The rule of law received more attention over a longer period of time, but progressively its content has been linked with the contents of 'human rights' and 'democracy' in the official discourse of the CCP.

The 'governing Party' is following a policy line of accelerated economic reform. This Party continues to subscribe to Marxist-Leninist 'democratic centralism' even while experiments with new formats of democratic governance that are supposed to widen citizen participation in the management of public affairs. The political system is no longer governed by Mao's imperative to facilitate class struggle. As Hu Jintao has put it, the revolutionary tasks of the early years are no longer relevant and 'governing' in response to the complexity of today's world involves a different set of political priorities and organizational opportunities.[14] The tasks of 'scientific development' are to be facilitated in a new division of labour that involves new and old organization and the opening of new channels of communication and participation.

Cognate rule of law, human rights and democratic reforms have fallen into place in a sequential fashion. Conceptually, if not practically, these three contents are increasingly interrelated, and entwined in a general synthesis of governance. However, while continuing to claim openness with respect to the best practice in the outside world, Chinese reform has deliberately sought a practical conceptualization and implementation of these contents on the basis of 'Chinese characteristics'. The strategy of reform is to move in deliberate increments and on the basis of reserved experiment rather than in a comprehensive all-fronts manner. The following analysis will attempt to trace the staged introduction of the contents of the rule of law, human rights and democracy and will hopefully establish an informed understanding of the origins, scope and depth of related reform.

The 'Rule of Law' in China?

There is a spectrum of conflicting opinion in the Western literature about the prospects for rule of law making in the particular context of China's political-legal system, *zhengfa xitong*.[15] As for the Party viewpoint, the CCP has often subscribed to the honest unity of words and deeds and the importance of sorting out the good and bad aspects of reality. On the other hand, the Party has politically urged its cadres to scale the heights. The Party's formal documentation does different things at different times. The 2005 White Paper on building political democracy was, for example, very candid about 'many problems yet to be overcome' that included problems of democracy in that 'the people's right to fully manage state affairs had not yet been fully realized'; and as for legal reform, 'laws that have already been enacted are sometimes not fully observed or enforced and the violations of the law sometimes go unpunished'.[16]

The 2008 White Paper on the recent historical development of the 'rule of law' in China did say that there are still problems, but, on the other hand, it claimed the following achievements:

> …China…has upheld the organic unity of CPC's leadership, the position of the people as masters of the country and law-based governance, stuck to the principle of people first, advocated the spirit of the rule of law, fostered the idea of democracy and rule of law, freedom and equality, fairness and justice, developed and improved the socialist legal system with Chinese characteristics, promoted the exercise of administrative functions in accordance with the law in all respects, deepened the reform of the judicial system, perfected the mechanism of restraint of and supervision over the use of power, guaranteed the citizens' lawful rights and interests, maintained social harmony and stability, and continuously promoted the institutionalization of all work.[17]

The establishment and continual development of the 'rule of law' is an ongoing struggle in any national context, but this is particularly true in China in light of the Confucian tradition that deliberately undervalued the importance of law and the subsequent revolutionary Party tradition that tended to put Party leadership and virtuous mass action above the law. The CCP created a 'political-legal system' (*zhengfa xitong*) that immediately politicized law to support the objectives and policies of the state and as ideologically subordinate to the CCP's political and ideological priorities, including the 'comprehensive management of public order' (*shehui zhi-an zonghe zhili*) since the late 1970s. The latter notion subordinates law within a wider campaign to generate law and order throughout society through the 'comprehensive' networking of all social and political organization.

Two issues or obstacles immediately stood in the way of the rule of law: tradition and party.

The 'Tradition' Issue

The Chinese tradition was a synthesis that included a continuously strong emphasis on Confucianism as well as a 'Legalist' emphasis on the state's use of law to further the purposes of the state. This approach assumed the law would reinforce the moral values established in the Confucian canon and in the ritualized relations of people in society. This law was utilitarian; it was mainly criminal law designed to facilitate severe punishment to ensure public order based upon deterrence.[18] 'Law' was not in any fundamental sense 'the touchstone of civilization'; it was a regrettable, but necessary stopgap to ensure compliance with imperial rule. The latter accepted the law's extended application in society as an inferior but absolutely necessary means of keeping social harmony through a system of rewards and punishments that were to reinforce the Confucian rationalized social hierarchy.

The active moral discrimination between right and wrong in the relations of people in social activity was considered a superior guarantee of any political order. Laws were bureaucratic phenomena. The Confucian official prided himself in his moral superiority. Such an official could not serve as some kind of 'utensil'. Government was not about measuring things with a yardstick, hence the famous aphorism, 'the superior man is not a utensil' (*junzi buqi*). Law did not have a natural dignity, nor did it produce the same benefit of internalized morality in the consciousness of people in society that was the case with demonstrated moral behaviour. The Son of Heaven's moral example was supposed to fly through the kingdom of China faster than his imperial writ. Moreover, 'litigation sticks', or lawyers made everyone pay without regard to justice and morality, hence the common wisdom: 'To enter a court of justice is to enter the tiger's mouth.'

The Party Issue

Mao Zedong flirted with anarchism in his youth, but he was certainly no anarchist as a leader. He disliked 'formalism', but conceded the necessity of rules while remaining extremely cautious about the organizational extremes of bureaucracy, or 'bureaucratism' (*guanliaozhuyi*). The initial CCP view of the law was, therefore, conflicted. What was of foremost importance to Mao Zedong and his Party was political organization and leadership that brings about changed attitudes and behaviour in the masses through education and struggle. At times his revolutionary impulse militated against the routine features of law. The latter were sometimes viewed as a reactionary constraint on the power of the people in making revolution. Moreover, under Mao's leadership, the CCP was ideologically predisposed to placing socialist morality directly within the substance of the law. Law was not above politics; it was part of politics. It was a weapon that could be used in class struggle, and on this basis 'policy' was even allowed to substitute for law. In Mao's day the Party subscribed to 'policy is the soul of law' (*zhengce shi falude linghun*). In the absence of actual law the Party State was free to fill in the blanks with improvised analogy.

Even now Mao's view of law as a project involving direct mass participation affects the position of law in the political system. Contemporary leadership focus on 'judicial democracy', *minzhu sifa*, values the collective consideration of crime and punishment and popular judgments offered by the 'people's assessors'. The ambivalence towards lawyers is still there. The system still includes direct participation of the people's assessors who sit alongside judges in court as well as collective decision-making by judges. This aspect has been re-emphasized in recent reform promoting 'judicial democracy'.

The mass line politics of Mao favoured simple down-to-earth law and disliked exclusive and privileged legal language that shut out the masses. The latter was denounced as a form of professional sectarianism. Mao's idea that the law should reflect the will of the people is still very important even today. During the Mao years, the law was a very deliberate matter of deterrence and education; it existed to protect society and to enshrine political objectives of Party rule. However, even under continuing Party rule, there have been significant changes that have directly challenged Mao's assumptions about the law.

Neither tradition nor Mao offered the law much respite. Under the reform leadership of Deng Xiaoping, however, the law became a key element in the plan for institutionalization that was designed not only to prevent future Cultural Revolutions, but also to further the 'four modernizations'. Deng hoped that the law's predictability, clarity and certainty would provide the basis for a 'rule-of-law economy' (*fazhi jingji*). Also, under Deng, the law in order to shore up political stability was increasingly associated with the protection of rights and interests. In reform theory the connection between rights and the subjective interests of members of society trumped past emphasis on obligations as superior to rights. These developments eventually paved the way for the introduction into China of 'human rights' law.

In the 1990s policy and jurisprudence placed new emphasis on the protection of rights, and this part of the Dengist institutionalization strategy addressed the destabilizing nature of fast socio-economic change. In future, law would help prevent the arbitrary politics of persecution that was so prevalent in the Cultural Revolution. This was why the new reform leadership needed not just a complete set of laws, but also the 'rule of law'. Deng's institutional strategy called for new governance in which the state would do everything according to law based upon the 'whole people grasping the law' as opposed to 'ruling the people by law'.

In the West the 'rule of law' developed as a means by which to contain the arbitrary exercise of power; law was needed to restrain the state. While the Confucian tradition showed little inclination to check the moral authority of the state, Deng Xiaoping and his veterans were very serious about using the law to prevent arbitrary politics such as had occurred in the class struggles of the Cultural Revolution. As they, themselves, had been victims of the kangaroo justice meted out by the masses, they placed a high priority on law. There were very strong political reasons why the Party endorsed the 'rule of law' as relevant to China.

At the Third Plenum of the Eleventh CCPCC in December 1978 Deng enunciated a position that later became the standard justification in reform advocacy of the 'rule of law'. The latter became a key element in the 'scientific' pattern of institutionalization that contrasted with personality cult. 'Act according to law' was a reaction to politics of leadership whim and constant political flux, hence Deng announced the following position:

> Democracy has to be institutionalized and written into law, so as to make sure that Constitutions and laws do not change whenever the leadership changes or whenever the leaders change their views.... The trouble now is that our legal system is incomplete.... Very often what leaders say is taken as law.... That kind of law changes whenever a leader's views change. So we must concentrate on enacting criminal and civil codes, procedural laws and other necessary laws. These should be discussed and adopted through democratic procedures.[19]

China's legal circles seized on Deng's new direction, arguing that the law had more stability than policy and that its predictability could obviate the uncertainties associated with the 'spirit of the leader'. One of China's most senior jurists, Zhang Yongming, was very clear on this point:

> In the past our work was often guided by our leader's spirit which might show inclination toward one orientation one day but the opposite...the next. Very often, some kind of intrinsically good 'spirit' could be freely interpreted by some people according to their own likes and dislikes.... In contrast, laws have the advantage of stability and cannot be changed at will.[20]

An important part of Deng's strategy for institutionalization related to the accelerated legislation of new law to replace the arbitrary politics of 'policy is the soul of law' (*zhengce shi falude linghun*). Reformers constantly recited his instruction: '...we need laws, these laws must be followed, their implementation must be strict, and violations of law; must be punished' (*you fa keyin, you fa biyi, zhi fa biyan, wei fa bijiu*). Policy could no longer serve in the absence of law; the laws had to be complete so as to control for arbitrary state policy and action.

This was not just a matter of 'rule by law' or traditional state legalism. The 'rule of law' was conceived as a means of reducing the spirit of the leader in Chinese politics. Wang Liming, a leading reformer, claimed in a national editorial, 'using law to rule the country' (*yifa zhi guo*) is not equal to 'the rule of law' (*fazhi*). 'Rule of Law' was articulated as an ethos; it was defined in its opposition to Cultural Revolutionary 'rule of man' (*renzhi*). As such it is an ethos that requires the law's supremacy and dignity vis-à-vis the unfair and fickle disposition of leadership that presumes that it is above the law and can wage class struggle against its enemies without any regard for due process and judicial justice. This new reform understanding was sanctioned in the wording of the 1982 state constitution:

> All state organs, the armed forces, all political parties and public organizations and all enterprises and institutions must abide by the Constitution and other laws. All acts in violation of the Constitution or other laws must be investigated.
>
> No organization or individual is privileged to be beyond the Constitution or other laws.[21]

This wording signalled a new formal interest in constitutionalism; however, the revision did not, itself, offer a means of ensuring the application of the Constitution's provisions. Also, Deng recognized the difficulties involved in anchoring the rule of law in both Party and public awareness. There was real concern that the Party would not let the law operate on its own cognizance, and there was a pattern of preempting the law in favour of applying Party discipline to Party members in trouble, hence the dilemma of 'substituting party discipline for the laws of the state' (*yi dangji daiti guofa*).

Deng raised these concerns directly with the Party Politburo in 1986:

> If the Party intervenes in everything, it will not help the people understand the importance of the rule of law. This is a question of the relations between the Party and the government, of the political structure of our country.... Right now the Party is concentrating on rectifying the conduct of its

own members, but at the same time we are trying to strengthen the rule of law in society at large. Our country has no tradition of observing or enforcing laws.[22]

Deng, himself, did not believe that the rule of law had a base in the Chinese tradition. His institutional strategy went ahead anyway, hailing a new set of core understandings and calling for rule-of-law education within the Party and among the people; however, this did not guarantee organizational consistency and new system-wide practice. At the same time as Deng emphasized the importance of a complete set of laws, there was a general Party focus on ensuring political stability after the Cultural Revolution.

For those responsible for social and political stability, the 'rule of law' posed a dilemma over means and ends. Reformers such as Wang Shengxuan argued: 'Only when everyone observes the law, can we promote socialist spiritual civilization and can we raise the people's communist morality.'[23] For others the law was just another method for ensuring the advance of 'socialist spiritual civilization'. The law was part of wider organizational strategy to ensure public order and stability; for example, the law was a tool to be used in the political struggle for the 'comprehensive management of public order' (*shehui zhi-an zonghe zhili*).[24]

The emphasis on 'comprehensiveness' harked back to past mass line strategy that insisted that all formal state and informal social organization should be integrated to achieve the Party's political goal of unity. Such comprehensiveness was needed to restore society and to deal with Cultural Revolution's impact on the family. The new emphasis on comprehensive management originated with an urgent focus on juvenile delinquency and crime that had been spawned in the Cultural Revolution attacks on family members for alleged 'capitalist restoration' and 'counterrevolution'.

The need for new Party understanding on the importance of the rule of law was emphasized in the revised wording of the Party Constitution that was approved in 1992:

[The Party] must conduct its activities within the limits permitted by the Constitution and law. It must see to it that the legislative, judicial and administrative organs of the state and the economic, cultural and people's organizations work actively and with initiative, independently, responsibly and in harmony.[25]

The new need for law became even more pronounced with the deeper progress of reform. In 1992, Deng's Southern Tour (*nanxun*) focused attention on 'the market economy is the rule of law economy' (*shichang jingji shi fazhide jingji*). Deng's Southern Tour theory effectively sanctioned the introduction of a market as the means of allocating resources. Under the planned economy, economic law merely confirmed whatever the state required as appropriate to its distribution of resources. The new market, however, required a predictable institutional framework that could handle competing interests.

Domestic events and political reasoning dictated the formal consolidation of the rule of law in China. In 1996, the Party endorsed Jiang Zemin's formulation, *yifa zhi guo, jianshe shehuizhuyi fazhi guojia*, 'running the country according to law and establishing a socialist rule-of-law country'. This same formulation was then incorporated directly into the State Constitution in an amendment of March 1999.

The Party, itself, took the lead in sponsoring the 'rule of law'. It did not see the latter as inherently opposed to its own leadership. The Party would guarantee the rule of law's proper development in Chinese conditions. 'Act according to law' (*yifa banshi*), required new recognition of the supremacy of the law, but this was presumably not a problem as whatever was formalized in law had already been vetted by the Party as the apparent reflection of the will and interests of the people and the new emphasis on law provides vital mediation of competing interests in society that can no longer be directly undertaken by the CCP, itself.

However, as Deng had indicated in 1978 for the new emphasis to develop in reality, China needed a 'complete set of laws'. There was massive legislation of law in the 1990s and even so the law was nowhere near complete. The showpiece for legal reform related to the major 1996–97 revisions to the 1979 Criminal Procedural Law and the 1980 Criminal Law. This reform was encouraging in that it expressly dealt with the issue of politics and supremacy of the law as it related to the age-old problem of 'policy is the soul of law' and cognate principles of analogy and flexibility; the revision promised a new rule of law regime based upon a commitment to the principle of legality.

In the past, the Party State used law for its own political purpose. This was even formally sanctioned in jurisprudential principles justifying analogy and flexibility. The 1996–97 reforms were especially focused on creating a 'rule of law economy'. There was related formal subscription to protection of rights and interests – this required 'balance of values' and 'protection of society' (*shehui baohu*) and 'human rights protection' (*renquan baozhang*).

Also, new emphasis was given to the procedural dimensions of protection of rights. It was acknowledged that previously the substantive dimensions of the Criminal Law had received most of the attention while the procedural dimensions of the Criminal Procedural Law languished. The latter needed equal status. Its objectives were as substantively important as the actual determination of criminal responsibilities in the Criminal Law. The idea of creating protective due process was very new and the system was biased against it. Procedural law therefore existed to facilitate public order on the basis of criminal law deterrence.

The 1996–97 revisions built on Deng's original instruction to ensure a complete set of laws. However, this revision prematurely assumed that indeed 'comprehensive stipulation' could cover all future development thus obviating the need for analogy and the substitution of policy for law. The revision embraced the fundamental 'principle of legality' as it is known in the West, 'no crime without a law'. The latter's corollary was also elevated, namely, 'no punishment without a law' in the struggle against the 'flexibility' of the *zhengfa* system. The reform also endorsed, at least in principle, if not consistently in the actual content of some of the new provisions, 'the punishment must fit the crime'.

Under Mao's assumptions, a discourse on the 'rule of law' in China was hardly possible. Collective leadership and reference to democratic centralism could not deal with the problems of personality cult and the spirit of the leadership negated the law as supreme in any case. The law was a weapon of class struggle. In the event that law stood in the way of mass mobilization and class struggle it was expendable. Deng and his successors assigned a more positive role to law in ensuring protection of 'rights and interests' (*quanyi*) in a rapidly changing society and economy.

The issues raised earlier with respect to tradition and to Mao's revolutionary line, are still important to an analysis of the prospect for contemporary legal reform. The key problem for the contemporary Chinese leadership is how to sustain the development of the rule of law in practice as an important element of 'democratic governance' in an entwined domestic and international context that calls for more transparency and accountability without fundamentally altering the position of the Party State. The latter represents the internal contradiction reflected in 'running the country according to law and establishing a socialist rule-of-law country'. China's political-legal system (*zhengfa xitong*) is a problematic Sinification; law is supposed to defer to the state and the political legal system generates reactive organizational and ideological tendencies that compete with emphasis on the law as the impersonal predicate in society and economy that defends equality before the law and confronts the politics of privilege.

Now the law is expected to take up the daily problems associated with new forms of competition and multidimensional nature of systems of ownership and distribution as these reflect the new 'contractual society' and as these forms reflect the new 'horizontal society' that is witnessing the development of 'newly emerging interest' in society. The related new emphasis on the protection of rights not only informs the purposes of China's 'socialist rule of law' but connects with new discourse on human rights in China.

A Chinese Human Rights Paradigm?

Is there a Chinese human rights paradigm? Those who focus on cultural relativism would say that the question is itself flawed in a contradiction in terms. 'Human rights' are supposedly universal in their essence. The Chinese, however, now argue that there is a legitimate synthesis of localization and internationalization in the formation, spread and development of human rights categories. At any rate, the Chinese adoption of human rights terminology is a significant political event, particularly given the absence of support in traditional Chinese culture and the Party politics surrounding the notion of 'human rights', as the latter were viewed as part of a hostile Western move to discredit Chinese socialism. Deng was initially a lot less accommodating on the question of 'human rights' than he was earlier on the 'rule of law'. In his view 'human rights' were closely tied to the issue of 'bourgeois liberalization' and 'peaceful evolution'.[26]

The Confucian tradition happily speculated on the potential morality in all human beings, but it did not contemplate human beings as individual rights bearing subjects primarily concerned with their own self-realization. The tradition offered some support for reciprocity as mutual obligation between moral subjects, but the latter were seldom equal and the focus was on obligations rather than rights, *per se*. Reciprocity primarily occurred between morally unequal subjects; it was not deployed to protect the rights of all subjects as equal members of society. This system of thought justified moral hierarchy and reciprocity was not aligned with a principle of equality.

The key issue was for the morally superior to instruct and mentor the morally inferior. Western sinology could argue that the traditional notion of '*li*' (decorum) confirmed the cosmological immanence of virtue throughout the world, but '*li*', translated variously as decorum, ritual and etiquette, whether it dealt with family members or on the relations of the Son of Heaven to princes, presumed hierarchy rather than equality and as 'ritual entered law', *li ru yu fa*, it reinforced a complexity of distinctions in the law's ascriptive response to rank and status. Confucianism made law, *fa*, bow to *li*, ritual, and hence it emphasized that 'good government relies on man', *weizheng zai ren*, and '*li*' is 'the way of ruling men' (*zhi renzhi dao*).[27]

Even Louis Henkin, a well known US expert on Chinese human rights law who argues that Confucianism can 'cohabit' with human rights, today acknowledges:

> Human rights are individual rights, dedicated to individual dignity; Confucianism might have found the focus on the individual, even on individual dignity, uncongenial. For Confucianism, the individual found dignity not in self-expression but in fulfilling the will of Heaven, not in individualism, but in membership in family, clan, community, not in equality but in mutual respect within an hierarchical order, less in law and legal remedies, administered by judges, than in the morality and compassion of rulers and officials.
>
> Confucianism did not seem to accept – as a principle – stated limitations on public policy or public interest out of concern for individual dignity, it relied on the wisdom and morality of rulers.[28]

The formal acceptance of 'human rights' into reform China was handicapped in the politics of ideological confrontation. During the 1980s, Deng Xiaoping opposed 'human rights' as he viewed them in the exclusively specious terms of a US-led 'human rights diplomacy' (*renquan waijiao*) that was part of a Western scheme of 'peaceful evolution', or 'disintegration' to destroy socialism from within and to make the regime change its colour.

Prior to 1991, Deng's leadership insisted on China's own concept of rights and obligations as these highlight 'citizens' rights' (*gongmin quan*). Deng's instinct was to reaffirm the legitimacy of the socialist state as it provides for rights through its own positive law, but this position was open to strident Western criticism that focused in Deng's insistence on positive law at the expense of rights that universally accrue to all participants in humanity.

In response to Western critics who characterized the Tiananmen Square 1989 event as a massive violation of human rights, Deng initially responded by arguing that in China political stability had to come before human rights and that the collapse of the regime would have resulted in a human rights crisis of monumental proportions:

As soon as they seize power, the so-called fighters for democracy would start fighting each other. And if a civil war broke out, with blood flowing like a river, what 'human rights' would there be? If civil war broke out in China, with each faction dominating a region, production declining, transportation disrupted and not millions or tens of millions but hundreds of millions of refugees fleeing the country, it is the Asia-Pacific region, which is at present the most promising in the world, that would be the first to be affected. And that would lead to disaster on a world scale.[29]

In the immediate aftermath of Tiananmen Square, Deng believed that the US had better apply the five principles of peaceful coexistence and not become involved with human rights and democratic rights in China.[30] Despite such strong reservations, the Chinese government eventually fashioned a new position – one that accepts a positive notion of rights in support of political stability and national development and one that helps promote China's extended relations with other countries and challenges international censure and trade sanctions.

Apparently Deng responded to reform argument that 'human rights' could be used to support domestic political and social stability in the context of rapid economic growth. Human rights identified and reinforced in domestic law offered some support in the context of the transition from the planned to the market economy. Workers, for example, who lost the constitutional guarantee of a lifetime of employment without dismissal need legislation guaranteeing the protection of their 'rights and interests' in the workplace. 'Human rights' were, thereafter, referenced in a new and extensive generation of national legislation concerning the protection of rights and interests in the 1990s and up to the present. Such legislation often referred to international experience and standards of social justice.

In what appears to be a very great victory for the reform explicit in 'seeking the truth from the facts', the Chinese position swung from 'human rights' are not legitimate, as they originated with an ideological campaign to smear China, to human rights are rights that should be developed everywhere as well as in China and that they should be correlated with the various interests in society that have to deal with consequences of the transition to the 'socialist market'. Moreover, the new policy promised gains at the international level. The previous focus on human rights as part of peaceful evolution had cut China out of the growing international politics discourse concerning the recognition of human rights categories and contents. The new policy got China a place at the table and was consistent with the new emphasis on more active participation in multilateralism.

With this new acceptance, over time there was convergence of the rule of law with human rights formation and application in Chinese policy thinking. This endorsement, however, was accompanied by continuing insistence on the struggle against 'bourgeois liberalization' and the rejection of specific contents concerning political rights relating to multi-party democracy, any notion of a bicameral legislature including a House of Regions and the separation of powers.

Key reformers such as Li Buyun could, however, freely support a definition of human rights that converged with mainstream Western definitions. Li equated 'human rights' with the 'modern rule of law state': 'The comprehensive and effective guarantee of human rights is not only the fundamental goal of the modern rule of law state, it is also the measure of such a society.' Li then defined 'human rights': 'Human rights are rights which ought to be enjoyed by virtue of human essence.'[31] New emphasis was consistent also with (a) new focus on the rule of law's approach to equality as opposed to the tyranny of rule of man, and (b) dropping of class struggle to focus on society as a structure of interests where rights protection is modern and rational in the context of a major socio-economic transition.

The way in which the rule of law and human rights were introduced suggested a changing relation between state and society, and the ongoing development of Deng Xiaoping's original strategy for post-Cultural Revolution institutionalization to promote political stability in the context of socio-economic transition to the marketplace. Despite the lack of relevant support in Chinese history and culture the 'rule of law' and 'human rights' language and legislation were introduced into China during a period of rapid change in China's political economy. Arguably, they were introduced as part of a reform strategy that was designed to facilitate national economic development and the new social contract of growth in return for political acquiescence in single-party rule.

Once Deng's regime accepted human rights terminology in late 1991 it subsequently became involved in a regular international exchange with the US on the topic of comparative human rights performance. Chinese analysis never failed to underline the relevance of sovereign equality and non-interference in the affairs of other countries as these 'bedrock' principles inform the UN Charter. China's own new human rights experts wished to be informed of the particular credentials that allowed the US to act as the exclusive 'global' judge and jury of other countries:

> At present, the United States is the only country which publishes a report every year to pass judgments, based on the concepts of value and human rights of its own upon human rights conditions in each of the more than 190 other countries and regions in the world. The US State Department has never justified itself for this....[32]

Chinese counterpoint claimed, for example, that the US State Department had misreported the differences between the two countries. The Chinese have disputed US claims that China was only interested in the rights embedded in the UN Covenant on Social, Economic and Cultural Rights and was not at all interested in civil and political rights. The first white paper on human rights set out the argument on the basis of the 'extensiveness' of 'human rights'. The latter term highlighted the fact that not just specific classes or social strata, but China's entire citizenry should enjoy human rights. The term also implied an 'extensive scope', 'including not only survival, personal and political rights, but also economic cultural and social rights'.[33] The range of rights, highlighted in Chinese constitutional law and China's greater acceptance of international treaties on human rights were featured in China's annual rebuttals to the US State Department.

Undoubtedly, China's international position places a great deal of stress on state sovereignty and a related principle of non-interference. Surprisingly or not, the 1991 White Paper on human rights conceded the possibility of international cooperation and intervention in domestic national affairs:

> ...the international community should interfere with and stop acts that endanger world peace and security, such as gross human rights violations caused by colonialism, racism, foreign aggression and occupation as well as apartheid, racial discrimination, genocide, slave trade and serious violation of human rights by international terrorist organizations.[34]

The Chinese shifted their paradigm accepting 'human rights' terminology as part of their own domestic and international thinking. They disavowed 'cultural relativism', claiming that while international norms do exist and that under certain circumstances the principle of non-interference may have to be qualified, human rights are legitimately understood and developed from within domestic societies.

There are as Qiao Keyu suggested 'internal correlations' and 'external correlations' and the former are more basic than the latter, but the latter have still to be factored into the overall analysis. The scholars in the 1990s in fact lobbied for human rights on the basis of a synthesis of 'localization' (*bentuhua*) and 'internationaliza-tion' (*guojihua*). 'Localization' as distinct from 'localism' was viewed as legitimate and to be distinguished from the Western critical focus on 'cultural relativism'. In 1998, Li Lin, for example, defined and reported on 'internationalization': 'Internationaliza-tion is the international developmental process in law in which the particular legal systems of each country in the world, approximate more closely and come together and converge in order to take shape in mutual interdependence and linkage.'[35] 'Localization', on the other hand, was viewed as the law's sensitive adaptation to the underlying values and understanding of distinctive society and political culture. Note that politically this kind of argument easily fits with reform argument that exalts 'socialism with Chinese characteristics'. National self-determination and international norms are often discussed as mutually supportive in the modern context of interdependence.

Not only Western human rights critics, but also Chinese leaders and jurists will say that there is obvious difference between subscribing to an ideal and actually adopting it in practice. Indeed the former Minister of Justice in China said that new law aspiring to bright new principles has to worry about 'customary practices'. In other words, officials have been used to doing things in a certain way, and they will need considerable new practice and thinking to deal with the new reform emphasis on the protection of 'rights and interests'.

Following upon formal acceptance of human rights terminology, there was a torrent of new legislation correlating 'rights' with 'interests' rather than 'obligations' and newly focusing on the protection of these rights. The following legislation is only a selective listing of a heavy national legislative agenda that dealt with the initial range of human rights categories: the Administrative Procedural Law of the PRC (4 April 1989); the PRC Law on Governing Assembly, Parade and Demonstration (31 October 1989); the PRC Law for the Protection of the Handicapped (28 December 1990); the Law of the PRC for the Protection of Minors (4 September 1991); the PRC Law on the Protection of Women's Rights and Interests (3 April 1992); the PRC Labour Law (5 July 1994); Law on Protecting the Rights and Interests of the Elderly (26 August 1996); Revised PRC Criminal Procedural Law (April 1996); Revised PRC Criminal Law (March 1997); Revised Marriage Law (March 2001).

It would take several volumes to examine and explain in detail all of the distinctions and vocabularies that have been introduced in rights-related legislation; however, the following analysis will focus on two key areas of potential change that demonstrate the cultural and institutional problems in introducing and applying human rights legislation in China.

The first example relates to human rights pertaining to personal rights and gender equality and it discusses in particular the 2001 revision to the Marriage Law which led to the criminalization of 'domestic violence'. This issue highlights the state's changing relationship to the family in law.

Secondly, one of the most difficult areas of reform concerns the organization of due process within the Chinese justice system. In the traditional context, there was little effort devoted to the protection of the individual against unfair process. And, as was mentioned, the Criminal Procedural Law which houses due process was for a long time underdeveloped and subordinate to the substantive concerns that were ideologically expressed in the criminal law. The 1996 revision to the CPL was especially instructive as it hastily introduced new American-style aspects of the adversarial, as distinct from inquisitorial process. In hindsight this turned out to be a case of good intentions gone awry.

The Criminalization of Domestic Violence

The rising pattern of domestic violence, both in the cities and countryside, was aggravated by the underlying dynamics of reform in the context of resurgent traditional values. Within the household, there was much more stress on the importance of male labour, and with the new law on women's rights and interests there were more arguments about who owns what. The integrity of the Chinese family concerned China's leaders and legislators. During the Cultural Revolution family members had been coerced into struggling against one another and this fostered a long-term rise in juvenile delinquency. In the context of economic reform and greater exposure to Western trends, there was new reform interest in phenomena such as domestic violence, rape within marriage and sexual harassment in the workplace.

Reformers took advantage of the 'political capital' that came with the Fourth World Conference on Women in Beijing. This conference's Action Guiding Principles included emphasis on dealing with domestic violence; and the conference filliped domestic and international liaisons on the subject of domestic violence (and to a lesser extent on sexual harassment) and developed local popular organization and lobbying that progressively focused on the problems of domestic violence.

Local reformers used UN standards in support of related new domestic law citing for example, the UN Declaration on the Elimination of Violence Against Women – a convention that Chinese human rights reporting had always noted had been signed by the Chinese government, but not the American government. The UN example discussed 'domestic violence' as 'violence against women…which has caused or will probably cause women pain in mind, body, and sex…no matter where it happens in public or private life'.

A victory of sorts occurred with the 2001 revision of the Marriage Law in that for the first time the law referenced 'domestic violence' (*jiating baoli*) as a 'crime'. National People's Congress (NPC) legislators responding to domestic understanding and mores, however, would not go as far as the UN and some of China's reformers. Domestic violence was limited to severe physical abuse and 'domestic violence' was not given the singular precedence demanded by reformers as it was placed in revised Article 3 together with 'bride-trafficking', 'mercenary marriage', bigamy and concubinage.[36]

Also, the NPC legislators steered clear of cognate emphasis on 'domestic violence' as sexual and psychological abuse.[37] Disappointed in their hopes of a standalone Article in the new marriage law, domestic reformers immediately regrouped, focusing with their NPC supporters on the drafting of new piece of national legislation on the exclusive subject of domestic violence.

Nevertheless, the 2001 revision was still very significant as it emphasized a strategy of state intervention, or 'countermeasure' by which the state would become proactive and involve itself directly in sensitive family relations to curb 'domestic violence'. In the traditional context, such sensitive matters seldom came into the formal justice system. Such an extremely sensitive issue was kept within the family as a 'private' matter.

The revision's countermeasures challenged the traditional distinction between public and private and called for state-led rights activism. However, the latter is evolving away from the exclusive authority dimensions of the 'comprehensive management of public order' that was predicated in monopoly of women's affairs under the Women's Federation under the democratic centralism of the CCP. The NGO, the Centre for Intervention against Domestic Violence, for example, is focusing alternatively on 'comprehensive community intervention' that includes wide international and domestic organizational liaisons connecting the Centre with the Federation, government departments, university research centres, international human rights agencies and sponsors and new domestic 'secondary organizations' that work in the same issue area.[38]

The Dilemmas of Procedural Justice

The 1996 revised CPL was a marvellous statement of reform. Its emphasis on due process challenged 'decide first, trial later' (*xianding, houshen*). It recognized the principle of legality as it pertains to 'no crime without a law' and 'no punishment without a law'. Exclusive reliance on heavy punishment as deterrence was also challenged in a new perspective requiring a 'balance of values' (*jiazhi pingheng*) that would, on the one hand, support public order and social stability, while, on the other, offer assistance to individuals who have very little means of defending themselves in the face of a monolithic state that considers itself as the custodian of political stability and social order. The revision was somewhat conflicted in its expansion of the death penalty categories for economic crime, but when taken as a whole the 1996–97 revisions to the CPL and CL mounted a new challenge to the tradition of heavy penalty-ism as it conflicted with 'the punishment must fit the crime' and the related key principle of 'equality before the law'.

The revision to due process moved in the direction of the adversarial system, but this reform was hasty and incomplete. The revision lacked a proper operational basis within a system that was organized on the exclusive basis of the inquisitorial system. The relations between prosecution, judges and defence needed much more discrete explanation and organizational detail. The laws of evidence remained inadequate. Reformers have since realized that there is the need for another major revision to sort out all of these problems.

The most recent White Papers show that there is ongoing political determination to support procedural reform that is consistent with the 1996–97 breakthroughs on the new importance of rights protection. The 2000, 2003, 2004 human rights White Papers all carried chapters on the 'Judicial Guarantee for Human Rights'. They also claim remarkable results in reform that are backed up with selective statistics. For example, the 2001 White Paper reported: 'In 2000 procuratorial organs throughout the country placed 4,626 criminal cases involving misconduct by judicial personnel on file for investigation according to law; put forward 14,349 rectification opinions against public security organs adopting improper mandatory measures and other law-violating actions.'[39]

The 2003 report was notable in that it gave new emphasis to problems of practice that concern 'judicial democracy' (*minzhu sifa*). In 2003, cases of extended detention concerning 25,736 people 'were corrected, basically rectifying such deviations' following the Supreme People's Court and Supreme People's Procuratorate and Ministry of Public Security jointly issued 'Notice on the Strict Enforcement of the Criminal Procedural Law and on the Conscientious Prevention and Correction of Extended Detention'. Similarly, 88,050 administrative lawsuits of 1st instance resulted in the annulling of 11.74 per cent of alleged improper administrative actions. There were, however, only 259 cases of illegal detention reported.[40] Over the last several years the legal community has been working on revisions to the 1996 CPL, and the Hu Jintao leadership is promising a major overhaul of all the key procedural laws by 2010.[41]

At the highest level of generalization, the development of human rights relevant legislation and related operating strategy was seen as part of the strategy of institutionalization. Problems in the community were to be overcome through 'acting according to law'. Every now and then the state's mistreatment of an individual does get public attention. The case of the beating to death of Sun Zhigang while in custody is particularly interesting in that it apparently led to the elimination of one of the most controversial categories of administrative detention, namely, 'custody for repatriation' (*shourong qiansong*).[42] In this author's opinion, however, while in legal circles reformers are quite interested in notions of due process, this is not likely the case with the majority of the population who are law-and-order inclined.

The 1991 paradigm shift that moved away from citizens' to human rights might even suggest that this issue is largely a matter of image, and this reflects on the question as to whether human rights legislation can have legs in Chinese society. Arguably the domestic reform process is maturing and is supported by a growing legal establishment within China. The question of image is not negligible. And definitely the relation to international standards can be used to facilitate reform, but the reform process has its own domestic dynamic and is not simply an artefact of international concern. Within the context of Party politics, the correlation of law and human rights has developed. The conscious incorporation of human rights into legislation is a serious domestic matter and not just a question of appeasing international publics.

Although image is very important, the real question is how to devise a political order or platform that would sustain the legitimacy of the regime's new social contract with the people. In the new era of governance, the 'governing Party' now stands politically committed to 'act according to law'. It is no longer so easy to resort to 'policy is the soul of law'. There are institutional consequences as well as the question of legitimacy that have to be considered.

In China, change is recognized at the highest symbolic level in amendment to the state constitution. The latter in China not only provides the nuts and bolts of governance, but it also sets out the latest Party thinking on where China is and where China is going. The rule of law and human rights were given the highest recognition by constitutional amendment in 1999 and 2004. The Party leadership may well have wished to use such milestones to demonstrate the convergence of 'localization' with 'internationalization' but, as is argued here, the emphasis on the protection of rights had also become part of the institutional strategy to ensure public order and social stability in the traumatic context of accelerated, deep and profound change in society. In this way, Chinese defined 'human rights' based upon the socialist Chinese rule of law was designed for purposes of political consolidation and legitimacy in a time of extraordinary uncertainty. This strategy was designed to sustain a political economy based on fast development.

The Prospect for 'Democracy' in China?

The greatest issue lies in the third content, that of democracy. For China's Western critics, the entire Chinese regime is coloured by its failure to adopt liberal democracy. Bruce Gilley, in his review of the future prospect for democracy in China, warns of 'Manicheans' who see China in terms of intractable autocracy, and he has also warned against 'misty-eyed Orientalists' who fondly anticipate 'some utopian synthesis of doctrines in China's future'.[43] The discussion here still insists, however, that we assess the aspects of 'democracy' that are now under review particularly in light of pragmatic Party understanding of the need for political restructuring to meet the future of economic growth and social instability.

The Chinese traditional political culture offered little support for the rule of law and human rights. The same is true for the conceptualization and development of 'democracy'. The emperor's 'subjects' were not rights-bearing human beings, but were part of a deliberately constructed moral hierarchy that was reinforced by rigid social etiquette and related law and familial convention. The official as *junzi* or 'superior man' preempted any need for representation as good governance was predicated in the provision of moral example by moral superiors. The Emperor's subjects were passively to accept without question such moral example. Moreover, absolute morality of imperial governance could not be questioned and opposition could not be accepted as constructive.

What does area studies say about the prospect for democracy in the Asian context? In his review, Robert Compton complains that Western social science 'treats culture as tautology that in the end explains nothing'. He focuses on the enduring relevance of several key aspects that often inform traditional Asian societies: the notion of a guardian class and related deference to authority that celebrates knowledge as the basis of moral guidance; the development of patron–client relations as hierarchical relations that bind superior and inferior together in 'mutual loyalty'; and the importance of group orientation that furthers cooperation based on inclusive moral consensus in processes of governance and socialization.[44]

In his well known book, *Developing Democracy*, Larry Diamond reviews Lucien Pye who sees 'Asian' political cultures as generally lacking in orientations that concern individualism and the healthy suspicion of authority. Pye viewed the prospects for liberal competitive democracy in Asia as limited. Diamond summed up this view as follows: 'Treating conceptions of power (and authority and legitimacy) as the crucial cultural axis for understanding alternative paths of political development. Pye identified common tendencies to emphasize loyalty to the collectivity over individual freedom and needs, to favor paternalistic authority relations that "answer deep psychological cravings for the security of dependency"; and therefore to personalize political power, shun adversary relations, favor order over conflict, mute criticism of authority and neglect of institutional constraints on the exercise of power....'[45] Pye has been criticized for determinism, but analysis should still take into account the difficulties of entrenching new ideas given the circumstances of tradition. Diamond acknowledges this in his review of political culture, but he also indicates that 'culture is not destiny'. In *Democracy in East Asia* he claimed: 'Over the next few decades East Asia is likely to be the most critical arena in the global struggle for democracy.' He also claimed 'a near consensus among our authors that culture is not destiny'.[46]

Also, Chinese analysis, itself, does not automatically assume that when tradition is taken into account that it is exclusively negative in its impact on reform. As mentioned in Chapter 2, even Mao was open to the positive aspects of past Chinese experience as well as foreign experience. Certainly an exclusive focus on tradition cannot explain why the CCP, since 1991, has experimented with and formalized particular correlations of rule of law, human rights and democracy.

Chinese 'democracy' suckled at the breast of Chinese nationalism. In the beginning it was merely a foreign instrumentality that nationalists believed could be conscripted to support China's 'wealth and power'. In the international context of competitive nationalism and Third World revolution 'democracy' attained an iconic salience in the politics of China. This third concept has in that sense deeper roots in contemporary political culture than was the case either with the rule of law or human rights. And yet it has only recently been receiving priority in national political discourse that is entwining the three concepts.

All along, Party nationalism has steadfastly refused to accept liberal democracy as a system to be replicated in China. The latter was a clever self-interested system of checks and balances that served only to protect pre-eminent private property interests. Its focus on Party-based elections distracted from the political manipulation of electoral democracy by a propertied elite class. 'Socialist democracy' was defined as an alternative that treated democracy as an essential element of the social system. This was reaffirmed in the tense circumstances of Tiananmen Square 'turmoil'. Deng was frustrated with student activists who set about to create a 'totally westernized vassalage bourgeois republic' (*xifangfu yonghuade zechanjieji gongheguo*).

The following *Beijing ribao* analysis drew upon established Party argument as to 'socialist democracy':

> By saying that socialist democracy needs to be developed and continuously improved, we certainly mean that there are still deficiencies in our socialist democracy at the present stage.... Some people who stuck to bourgeois liberalization thought that they could take advantage of this. They blatantly attacked our political system and described it as something without merit.... They took capitalist democracy as the sole yardstick and denounced everything varying from capitalist democracy as non-democracy.... The questions we want to ask are, In what scope do the majority of people exercise their rule? How do we determine whether things are decided according to the interests and will the majority of the people?[47]

Party analysis re-emphasized the differences between 'socialist' and 'capitalist' democracy in light of the alleged political confusion of Tiananmen Square dissidents.

Party analysis asserted: 'Capitalist democracy suits capitalist private ownership.' It claimed: 'Capitalist democracy is a kind of democracy in which the minority rules over the majority.'[48] The competitive system of elections is assumed to be an elaborate smokescreen for elite politics. Elections are controlled by moneyed elites. Tiananmen Square counterrevolutionaries such as Wan Runnan, Yan Jiaqi and Wuer Kaixi were out to turn themselves into a democratic elite:

> Who will pay the expenses? Probably only the 'elite' of the turmoil like Wang Runnan, Yan Jiaqi, Wang Dan, Wuer Kaixi and so on can participate in the election campaign, because they have money and are idle. When they do not have enough money their foreign bosses can subsidize them. Once our state power is in their hands, they will naturally pursue 'elite' politics, or 'elite' democracy.[49]

In 1989, Deng's Party claimed that it would protect the interests of the overwhelming majority of the Chinese people. What has changed since? The first White Paper on 'political democracy' appeared under the leadership of Hu Jintao in October 2005. The paper's first section, entitled 'A Choice Suited to China's Conditions', stated: 'The goal of the CPC's leadership of the people (for the people) is to realize democracy for the overwhelming majority of the people, and not just for a minority of the people.'[50]

The White Paper reflected Mao's original perspective on learning. It objected to 'mechanically copying the Western bourgeois system', but it claimed an open-minded development of a Chinese concept of democracy that would not only emphasize China's own experience and wisdom, but would take into account a variety of foreign sources and experience:

> China has always adhered to the basic principle that the Marxist theory of democracy be combined with the reality of China, borrowed from the useful achievements of the political civilization of mankind, including Western

democracy, and assimilated the democratic elements of China's traditional culture and institutional civilization.[51]

The distinction between capitalist and socialist democracy was reiterated to associate the Party with the overwhelming majority of the people and the protection of their interests under 'people's democratic dictatorship' but in the last paragraph of Section One there was an interesting caveat, or qualification to the effect that 'the majority be respected while the minority is protected'. The White Paper referred to the grave mistakes of the Cultural Revolution (1966–76). This same paragraph criticized 'democracy for all' as in opposition to the collective good. This formulation conjured up the extreme left's use of 'great democracy' (*daminzhu*) in the Cultural Revolution to persecute large numbers of people who were deprived of their rights and arbitrarily treated as counterrevolutionaries. Apparently, they had caused trouble in exercising 'four freedoms' (*sida ziyou*) that gave the masses their head allowing them to use the media for the airing of their views, the writing of big-character posters, great debates and extensive contacts to supervise the Party and government. The Cultural Revolution and then the experience of Tiananmen Square in 1989 placed a premium on the importance of political stability and the need to exercise vigilance in relation to calls for such 'extensive democracy'.

Hu Jintao admonished many in the CCP for having failed the people in their leadership. Seeing the spread of corruption and the deterioration of party organization, Hu strongly advocated a return to first principles – the Party was instructed to keep in touch with the feelings of the masses and to 'put the people first'. Still smarting from the encounter with SARS and the initial problems associated with organization and the lack of transparency and proper reporting, Hu organized a Party decision on governance that was unusually pointed in its direct attacks on Party members for their failed leadership:

> Our party has been steeled into a more mature and stronger party in practice, and the party's ability to govern is generally compatible with the heavy tasks and mission that it shoulders. However, in the face of the

new situation and tasks, the party's leadership and governance methods, leadership setup, and work mechanisms are not perfect, the ideological and theoretical level of certain leading cadres and leadership groups is not high, their ability to govern according to law is not strong, they have little skill in resolving complex contradictions, and their quality and ability are incompatible with the, but demand for implementing the important thinking on 'Three Represents' and comprehensively building a well-off society.[52]

It was this type of thinking that informed the new emphasis on the 'governing Party' (*zhizheng dang*).

The connotations of 'democracy' are changing, but the change has more to do with the refurbished Party techniques of engaging the masses than it has to do with a new push for 'legislative democracy'. Socialism may no longer require the defeat of the class enemy in large-scale class struggle, but the Party needs to promote a more effective management of public affairs so as to ensure a framework appropriate to continued economic success. This leaves the gate open to some consideration of 'good governance' in terms of focus on accountability, transparency and wider participation and/or consultation with respect to public policy-making.

New Party energy had to be directed towards leading the people to manage the state. The Party was to lead:

... the people to practice grassroots democracy and manage their own affairs in accordance so as to enable them to exercise self-management, self-education and self-service through democratic elections, democratic decision-making, democratic management and democratic supervision. Such a task also required the Party to lead the people to manage their own affairs in accordance with law.[53]

Moreover, reference to the 'rule of law' emphasized the key importance of the protection of human rights.

The 2005 White Paper sought to describe several democracies including 'government democracy' which it defined as 'effective participation by the masses in government decision-making'.

The government was charged with appropriate enforcement of the law:

> In the course of enforcing the law, attention has been placed on protecting the legitimate rights and interests of the parties concerned and the parties of interest, and on resolutely rectifying misconduct that encroaches on the interests of the people, abuse of power for personal gain and other breaches of the law, so as to ensure the laws are enforced in a strict, just and civilized manner.[54]

Beyond this issue of enforcement, however, there was a 'pragmatic' emphasis on a new pattern of responsibility requiring more direct engagement of citizens in administration:

> Guided by the principle that things that can be handled by citizens, legal persons, or other organizations independently, or be regulated by the market competition mechanism, or be solved by industrial organizations or intermediaries through self-disciplinary mechanism, shall not be solved through administrative ways by administrative organs, the relations between government and enterprise, government and the market, and government and society have been rationalized gradually, and things that government need not bother about shall be shifted to enterprise, the market or society accordingly.[55]

This extends the earlier Hainan reform strategy of 'small government, big society'. While no doubt the Party would determine what tasks would be offloaded to the masses, this strategy implies more than 'consultative paternalism' and envisages a new participatory division of labour in China's modern society and economy.

Referring to the key importance of 'governing Party', Brantly Womack has explored the distinction between 'legislative democracy' and 'Party democracy'.[56] Under Hu, the electoral development at the basic levels has continued, but there has not been an extension of direct constituency elections to the provincial or central levels. The people's congress system at the provincial and national levels is still in essence an appointment process rather than an electoral process; however, the point is well worth considering whether, under the rubric of 'socialist democracy', it is still possible to develop new formats of public participation as well as consultation.

This seemed to be the point behind Hu Jintao's 15 October 2007 remarks at the 17th National Party Congress:

> The essence and core of socialist democracy are that the people are masters of the country. We need to improve institutions for democracy, diversity its forms and expand its channels, and we need to carry out democratic elections, decision-making, administration and oversight in accordance with the law to guarantee the people's rights to be informed, to participate, to be heard, and to oversee.[57]

The issue of democracy was again featured in 2008. The Mayor of Taizhou, Chen Tiexiong, was, for example, inspired by the inclusion of the 'enterprise-established collective wage consultative system' in Premier Wen Jiabao's March 2008 government work report. The Mayor pinned his hope for industrial harmony on a wider democratic forum for negotiation between all possible parties.

In addressing the issues in the Premier's report, Li Junru, Vice-Presdient of the Central Committee Party School, discussed 'democracy' in a more general and perhaps substantive manner. Predictably Li stressed that political structural reform is very complex and it must respect China's own history and conditions. He bluntly argued that China should not be judged in such an exclusive manner with respect to elections.

Li candidly stated:

> In recent years, the political science discipline in the west has been swept with a research craze on 'deliberative democracy' theories and this is where the key reason lies. Election (ballot decision) democracy of the past, which was the core of traditional Western democracy, can no longer satisfy the people's increasing democratic demands today. – The democracy sought by China is the democracy of the genuine majority. What is being sought is actual equality, rather than its external form. Democracy must be realized not only within the political realm, but also in the economic domain.[58]

Western analysis tends to view the deliberative model of democracy as one featuring elected assemblies, but Li focuses on deliberation in other formats throughout society. Li distinguished three democratic forms including ballot decision by election 'deliberative-style democracy' whereby citizens express their will through consultations and then a collective will is to be executed by the government and the citizens collectively. This notion of citizen involvement in execution suggests convergence with the 2005 white paper as it explained 'government democracy'. The third form, Li indicated, was 'negotiation' whereby stalemated political forces are required to sit down to negotiate their respective interests.

Just in case we might have missed the point, the Vice-President of the Chinese Academy of Social Sciences, Zhu Jiamu, seconded Li, drawing on the Mao/Deng emphasis on learning through 'seeking the truth from the facts' to rebuke those whose minds were bent on copying the Americans:

> ...whenever some people discuss democracy, their minds will be filled with the American form and will take it as a benchmark. This indicates a failure of emancipating the mind and this is a new doctrinism, neo-conservatism and new restrictive framework. ...it is necessary to establish China's democratic concept and take China's democratic path.[59]

Indeed, under Hu Jintao's fourth generation of leadership there is renewed emphasis on 'democracy' in the PRC, but this is in contradistinction to embracing liberal democracy. Beyond the matter of elections, reform under the 'governing Party' has articulated more explicit correlations of the rule of law, human rights and democracy. This represents the top of a cycle of reform that has been carried out on the basis of Party leadership and organization.

The Contradictions of Sinification

The principal contradiction in China today is the Party's leadership and identification with China. In his recent assessment of the CCP's chances of survival David Shambaugh noted that there were more tendencies towards Party atrophy than adaptation. His analysis seriously doubted the possibilities of 'Western-style democracy' taking root in China; however, Shambaugh also disagreed with assumptions that China had reached a 'tipping point' at which there would be either a 'revolution from below or democratic breakthrough from above'. Even given significant evidence of atrophy, Shambaugh argues that the CCP '…remains a nationwide organization of considerable authority and power'.[60]

This chapter has reviewed the reform connection between the rule of law, human rights and democracy. The Party, itself, has sponsored these essentially Western concepts while maintaining its leadership over a profoundly complex and deep transition in China's economy and society. That concepts such as the rule of law, human rights and democracy have been introduced in form, if not always in consistent practice is, itself, rather incredible given the utter lack of support for these contents in the Chinese traditional political culture. The Party has reiterated its own importance to the rights and interests of the overwhelming majority of the people. This basis of authority has little to do with China's deep past, but a lot to do with the history of modern Chinese nationalism. As a paradox of modern Chinese nationalism the Party is all the more puzzling given that it is at the epicentre of corruption, and still has led one of the most extraordinary economic transitions in the history of modern nation-building.

Henry Kissinger had once explained that it is not possible to introduce 'human rights' into a 'totalitarian', as distinguished from an 'authoritarian', national context, for the totalitarian system by definition is characterized by a single ideology that pervades all of society and is at all levels organized through pervasive networks of Party-led social and political organization. The system cannot evolve as there is no freedom of thought and no related organizational creativity.

Such assumption is not helpful in understanding China today. Can we understand Chinese success or failure on the basis of human rights monitoring of China's changing conditions such as that undertaken by Freedom House? The latter's annual survey self-describes its assumptions as liberal democratic. Freedom House evaluates categories of civil and political rights. It is not interested in the claims of an alternative 'socialist democracy' that features 'democracy' as within society. Freedom House treats those rights featured in the UN Covenant on Social and Economic Rights as secondary and aspirational rather than primary and substantive.

As has been shown, Chinese analysis heartily disagrees with such assumption and believes that how 'democracy' connects with society relates to the essence of China's 'socialist democracy'. China's Freedom House rating has not budged over the years and despite the extraordinary changes that have come with reform, including massive reduction in absolute poverty, China, however, is still slotted together with North Korea, Cambodia, Myanmar and Iran as the 'worst of the worst' in the Freedom House ratings.[61]

In fact Larry Diamond recently featured Arch Puddington's Freedom House survey in his *Foreign Affairs* assessment of the contemporary rollback of liberal democracy at the international level. The two authors agree that the rollback in contemporary democracy is due in part to the backward nature of large recalcitrant states such as Russia and China.[62] Apparently, these states have helped delay the end of history.

But what are we to make of the China difference? The CCP claims that its legitimacy lies in its capacity to achieve developmental success on the basis of Chinese praxis. Chinese Marxist-Leninist Party praxis is fostering a state-led activism in establishing human rights based upon the Chinese socialist rule of law and democracy. The CCP may dwell on its credentials as the only true exponent of modern Chinese nationalism, but at the same time it has opened China's door wide to essential foreign concepts and institutions.

Is the CCP one of Compton's 'Asian' guardian elites that require public deference in light of their self-appointed task of protecting the Chinese community? Although Mao did not want to 'lop off Chinese history', Mao Zedong Thought had clearly attacked the Chinese tradition in so far as it imposed an absolute morality on politics. Such imposition denied the collective creativity and wisdom of the masses. Also, Mao Zedong Thought specifically supported dialectical learning based on the theory of contradictions, and this was key to Deng Xiaoping's political strategy to develop new institutions and related concepts that could withstand the tensions associated with fundamental socio-economic change and at the same time preempt any tendency towards future class struggle and cultural revolution.

In his expert testimony to the US Congressional Executive Commission on China, Jonathan Hecht, a leading Yale expert on due process and human rights in China, advised on the need to monitor China's legal developments: 'However, paradoxical as it may seem, law is simultaneously the principal medium through which Chinese are engaging in debate and experimentation about human rights and the closely related issues of the predictability, transparency, and accountability of state action.'[63]

The 'rule of law' was an essential component of Deng's institutional strategy for controlling the 'spirit of the leader', or the personality cult of Mao Zedong. Deng also wanted law to protect 'rights and interests' so as to achieve social and political stability in the heady context of rapid economic transformation. Particularly in the advent of the 'three represents' of Jiang Zemin, the Party focused on the 'adjustment of interests' (*quanli tiaozheng*) during accelerated reform. In theory the Party placed itself under the rule of law, but it assumed the guardianship of the rule of law. Moreover, the Party abandoned positive law and the exclusive focus on 'citizens' rights', but then proceeded to prioritize the development of categories of human rights within a new generation of legislation that sought to materialize 'rights and interests' in a fast-changing society. Law, human rights and democracy are now all featured in Hu Jintao's 'scientific development concept' that focuses on the building of a 'harmonious society' in China.

Moreover, when Hu Jintao articulated the notion of a 'ruling party' he made a telling observation: 'It is not easy for a proletarian political party to seize power, and still less easy for it to hold on to power, and especially over a long period. The party's governing status is not congenital, nor is it something settled once and for all.'[64] Under Hu the connotations of 'democracy' continue to develop. 'Democracy' requires the materialization of the will of the majority and the protection of rights and interests. The latter is seen as a matter of the newly inspired management of public affairs so as to ensure a framework appropriate to continued economic success.

Under 'Government Democracy' Hu's 2005 White Paper refers to the 'effective participation by the masses in government as 'grass roots democracy' builds upon a principle of 'equality before the law', and with the development of new organizational forms the people are expected to 'carry out self-administration, self-education and self-service'. This would seem to involve not only 'consultation', but also action based upon deliberation within a new organizational pattern of state–society relations. In other words, contemporary democratic reform insists that 'good governance' must include both consultation and wider participation in public policy making. There is no commitment in this to US-style elections but this direction seems to move way beyond the limitations of Chinese 'paternalism'.[65]

The sequence of reform connecting the rule of law, human rights and socialist democracy has been politically managed by the CCP largely for its own political purposes of continued economic growth and development on a viable institutional basis of political stability. The institutional supports for this economy have reflected elements of continuity and discontinuity. The rule of law, human rights and democracy have been conscripted in the cause of national economic development. This process, however, does have real implications in terms of the moderation of the conventional features of the one-party state. And Hu Jintao has pointed to the need for a deeper process:

> Socialist democracy has continued to develop and we have made steady progress in implementing the rule of law as fundamental principle, but efforts to improve democracy and the legal system fall somewhat short of the need to expand people's democracy and promote economic and social development and political structuring has to be deepened.[66]

4

'SOCIALISM', OR 'CAPITALISM WITH CHINESE CHARACTERISTICS'?

There is a metaphorical river that runs through China. On one river bank there is 'socialism', and on the other, 'capitalism'. Apparently Deng Xiaoping, when he introduced economic reform and the open door in late 1978, wanted to get across to the 'socialist' bank by 'groping the stones on the river bed' (*mozhe shitou, guohe*). Pop songs of the 1980s playfully caricatured the resulting confusion. Apparently Deng was so busy groping for the stones on the bottom of the river bed that he forgot to look up to see which side of the river he was heading for. How have Deng and his successors defined 'socialism' and how far has China moved away from socialism towards capitalism?

There is a key problem of historical perspective that originates with popular understanding of the history of post-1949 China. At the Third Plenary Session of the Eleventh Central Committee in December 1978 Deng Xiaoping shifted Party line away from class struggle and towards the 'four modernizations'. Ever since, economic reform and the open door have been justified within the Party on the basis of reference to the Third Plenary Session of the Eleventh Central Committee. Also, in Western historiography, December 1978 has been taken as the starting point of an entirely new line or approach to political economy.

It would be easy to boil down the course of Chinese politics suggesting that before 1978 China was about Mao's revolution and after 1978 China was about Deng's modernization. Deng's pragmatism is then neatly contrasted with Mao's fixation with revolution, and in 1978 China begins to practise a new diplomacy abroad and pragmatic modernization at home. Party historiography has not entirely agreed with a strict chronology that separates pre- and post-1978 into watertight compartments. Deng's banner has been held high by succeeding leaders, and there has also been an emphasis on the continuity represented in 'four generations' of continuous leadership.

Deng generated a new Party consensus on the importance of experiment that was legitimated in past policy and ideology. This disarmed the left while encouraging a new regime of experiment in the economy. Deng's 'great experiment' deliberately dealt with discontinuity from within continuity. Deng selectively borrowed from CCP policy history and Mao Zedong Thought to justify his 'second revolution' as a 'great experiment'.

The idea of experiment originated with the 1940s 'Yan'an Way'. Based on Mao's dictum, 'seeking the truth from the facts', the Yan'an Party had responded so well to the realities of border region society and economy that the senior American diplomat, John Service, characterized the Party's pragmatism as an equivalent to Western social science. All ideas were subject to debate as the Party responded to the 'three alls' of the imperial Japanese army and the Guomindang blockade.

Secondly, the 'open door' idea developed out of the Party debates of 1956, as analysed in Chapter 2. Mao warned against both 'blind Westernization' and 'dogmatism' and proposed a critical dialectical approach to the learning of the 'strong points' of all countries and cultures.

Thirdly, the four modernizations and particularly the approach to material incentives in the countryside connected with policy experience of early 1960s economic reconstruction. The reform notion of the household contract responsibility system built upon the early 1960s downloading of decision-making to the household.

Deng launched the 1978 economic reform with the re-circulation of Mao's 1956 blueprint for development, 'On the Ten Major Relationships'. He also emphasized that the 1956 Eighth National Party Congress had originally set out 'correct policies' that confirmed the completion of the 'socialist transformation of private ownership of the means of production'. The

Party had then focused on 'the principal contradiction' between 'growing material and cultural needs of the people and backward production', but this line was lost in the subsequent 'twists and turns' of leftist politics. Deng then affirmed that the Party 'returned to its correct politics' at the Third Plenary Session of the Eighth Central Committee in 1978.[1]

Certainly, Deng Xiaoping reacted to the brutal politics and related ideological extremism of the Cultural Revolution. Unlike Mao he focused on 'leftist' rather than 'rightist' mistakes. Unlike Hua Guofeng, who facilitated between left and right, Deng was politically straightforward. Deng, unlike Hua, repudiated the Cultural Revolution and its line, 'class struggle is the key link'. Deng reacted against the extreme language and gross destructive behaviours of Cultural Revolutionary struggle. Deng had been accused of being a 'capitalist roader' who in his opposition to Mao's 'self-reliance' acted as a 'slavish comprador' who would turn China into a sweat shop for the imperialist powers. Deng responded by highlighting the correlation of 'independence and self-reliance' with the 'open door'.

Protesting his loyalty to Mao Zedong Thought, Deng used this thought to discredit Hua as Mao's successor; Hua had denigrated Mao's Thought when he idolized the Chairman with the notion of 'two whatevers'. Hua had misrepresented whatever the Chairman had said or directed as an absolute truth. 'Feudal culture' and the Cultural Revolution were based on the latter. At the Third Plenary Session, Deng deliberately contrasted the 'two whatevers' with 'We must emancipate our minds and use our heads.'[2] Referring to Mao's Thought, Deng created a discourse on the importance of 'liberating the mind', 'seeking the truth from the facts' and 'practice is the sole criterion for understanding the truth' that would allow for a focus on experiment within China's political economy.

He introduced a new rule in Party life, namely no more such extreme debates and 'empty-headed talk'. During one of his Southern tours, Deng noted that there had been no coercion or mass movement to consolidate the line of the Third Plenary Session, Eleventh Central Committee, for he had issued an instruction:

'...not to engage in a debate is my invention. By not engaging in a debate, we can spare more time for doing practical work. We must boldly conduct experiments and boldly break through.'[3]

His gritty style and strategy of leadership emphasized getting things down, but only on the basis of Mao's ideological emphasis on 'seeking the truth from the facts'. The cat theory was hurled against Deng in bitter polemics about the original *sanzi yibao* formulation that downloaded production decisions to the rural household and allowed for the extension of private plots, private enterprise and free markets. Deng truly did not care whether a cat is white or black as long as it caught mice, but what Deng regarded as legitimate policy difference, the 'left' magnified into a division between 'capitalism' and 'socialism'. Deng liked that part of Mao that had talked up learning as opposed to dogmatic copying. He agreed with Mao on the need to reduce 'formalism' that required too many meetings and repetitious speeches. He too subscribed to 'saying less and doing more'.[4] Deng wanted action through experimental praxis.

Deng had been personally accused of 'economism' and of practising a 'theory of productive forces' (*shengchanli lilun*), where he only focused on the importance of material incentives and ignored the political importance of class consciousness generated in class struggle within the arena of 'productive relations'. While Deng saw himself as advancing the cause of socialism through production increase, his enemies must have wondered whether this line did constitute what the 'gang of four' had reviled as the 'theory of productive forces'. The former was at the heart of so-called 'capitalist restoration' in the leftist polemics of the Cultural Revolution.

In December 1978 the final communiqué of the CCP Central Committee indicated its 'decision to close the large-scale nationwide mass movement to expose and criticize Lin Biao and the "gang of four" and to shift to...socialist modernization'. The 'four modernizations' were hailed as 'the greatest historic task of the time'. The Third Plenary Session, Eleventh CCPCC then promised to prepare the way for a major statement on Party history since 1949.

This summation was finalized in the 27 June 1981 'Resolution on Certain Questions in the History of Our Party'. The basic assumptions of the Resolution paved the way for the emphasis on the 'four modernizations'. The Decision debunked the Cultural Revolution. It concluded that China's 'socialist transformation' had already been completed before the Cultural Revolution. Secondly, the Cultural Revolutionary insistence on continuous struggle against 'capitalist restoration' and revisionism was 'the confusing of right and wrong'. 'Many things that were denounced as revisionist or capitalist during the "cultural revolution" were actually Marxist and socialist principles....' The left had misused Mao's mass line in its wholesale attack on Party leadership as the extension of the so-called 'new bourgeoisie'. Also the left had failed to apply Mao's dialectics in their assessment of the real situation in Chinese politics and society. They were 'metaphysicians' who had conjured up in their own heads a notion of the new bourgeoisie creating 'capitalist restoration'.[5]

In other words, the true defenders of socialism had been beaten up on a trumped up charge of 'capitalist restoration', and their opponents who were poor dialecticians sacrificed the well-being of the Chinese people for their own power and ambition. Deng's focus on production was for socialist and not capitalist purposes. His 'seeking the truth from the facts' originated in Mao Zedong Thought and was consistent with the scientific notions embedded in Mao's theory of contradictions. The Decision certainly gave Deng a great deal of satisfaction. It essentially agreed with Deng's earlier argument as it was broadcast in the 1973 'On the General Program of the Work of the Whole Party and Whole Nation'.

The latter had complained of 'bold elements' (i.e. leftists) who attempted to perpetuate the Cultural Revolutionary line on 'continued exercise of the dictatorship of the proletariat over the bourgeoisie'. In the final stages of Cultural Revolutionary polemic, the 1973 Decision had warned against the 'left': 'A Communist must see through sham Marxist political swindlers, one must not only look at their declarations but also at their concrete actions', and claimed: 'Some comrades are still using metaphysics in dealing with the relationship between politics and economics and between revolution and production…. They talk only about politics and revolution but not about economics and production.'[6]

Reform Strategy

In conventional Chinese Marxist-Leninist terms the distinction between 'capitalism' and 'socialism' lies in what are widely believed to be fundamental differences of the ownership and distribution systems. Agricultural modernization was one of the four modernizations. Deng's rural reform extended the principles of the early 1960s, especially as they related to *sanzi yibao*. Decision-making was shifted downward to the household. Eventually the Communes were dismantled. Formally, this was not 'decollectivization' although this term was often used in Western observation. The most important means of production, the land remained in the hands of public ownership. In the early 1960s there had been limited expansion of private plots and private trade fairs as supplementary to the collective economy in the countryside. Deng's economic reform experimented much more widely with the market although at first commodity production was seen only as supplementary to the planned economy. Under Deng there was a progressive relaxation of price controls and a graduated introduction of the market. The latter was at first represented as supplementary and the commodity economy was treated as a secondary phenomenon that would assist in the primary stage of socialism to provide more access to commodities to raise the standard of living.

China in the 'Primary Stage of Socialism'

In pushing for reform Deng pushed China back in ideological time. The left had been guilty of advancing too quickly in time, trying to generate a 'wind of communism' in the absence of appropriate material base in China's economy. This was adventurist politics that lacked a basis in 'seeking the truth from the facts' and which ignored the importance of economics and economic laws.

The influential reform economists such as Xue Muqiao and Sun Zhifang, rushed to flesh out Deng's argument that China was only in 'socialism' as the 'primary stage of communism'. Building on the repudiation of Gang of Four in 1981 Resolution on Party History, Xue, for example, accused the 'theoretical brains' of the Gang of Four, Zhang Qunqiao, of attempting to generate a 'wind of communism'. Zhang had given unqualified emphasis to politics ignoring the base and economic laws. Xue believed that China was only in a 'primary stage' given its low level commodity production, and the need for a higher standard of education and political consciousness throughout China's large population. There were insufficient productive forces to sustain communism based upon each according to his needs whereas under socialism there will be some tolerable distinctions based upon each according to his work. Under reform, highly specialized talent that made truly exceptional contributions to the national economy were to receive improved salary and work conditions. His analysis, based upon 'seeking the truth from the facts', revealed that prevailing conditions were not ripe for a dramatic acceleration towards Communism. Communism was pushed far in the future as China moved back into the 'primary stage of socialism'.

'Socialism' versus 'Capitalism' in Tiananmen Square, 1986 and 1989

Very few Western observers anticipated the trajectory of events towards *daluan* or 'great turmoil' in Tiananmen Square in the spring of 1989 when the mounting contradictions of reform resulted in massive demonstrations that shook the foundations of Party leadership. The road to Tiananmen Square, 1989 was littered with contradictions, but this road had been effectively foreshadowed in 1986.

In reacting to the Cultural Revolution and in defence of his economic reform and open door, Deng had concentrated ideologically on the threat underlying leftist adventurism. By the mid 1980s, however, he was becoming increasingly alarmed about the impact on society that came with the 'open door'. More than 'flies' were coming through China's door. Deng, on 7 March 1985, noted: 'Some people are worried that China will turn capitalist. You can't say that they are worried for nothing'. On 28 March 1986 Deng acknowledged that the 'open door' 'will inevitably bring into China some evil things that will affect our people'. At that point he was still optimistic that the Party would 'solve this problem by means of law and education'.[7] But he insisted on highlighting the negative connotations of 'liberalization', arguing that there was no such thing as 'socialist liberalization'.

Then on 28 September 1986, Deng, with growing impatience, warned the Central Committee that 'liberalization' is by nature 'bourgeois' and that 'there is no such thing as socialist liberalization'. The open door had raised the issue of socialism versus capitalism. Deng of course had, himself, identified with Mao in advocating a dialectic of learning from all countries, including the capitalist ones, but the difficulties of doing this were becoming critical as people inside and outside the Party were worshipping Western capitalist 'democracy' and 'freedom' at the expense of the Party and its 'socialist with Chinese characteristics'. Deng did not repudiate the open door, but he placed greater emphasis on 'relying on ourselves'. The useful things from the outside world were to be brought into China on the basis of critical Chinese Marxist understanding of the difference between 'right' and 'wrong'.

Deng believed that the Party would have to struggle for the next ten to twenty years against such insidious 'liberalization':

> If we fail to check this trend, it will merge with undesirable foreign things that will inevitably find their way into China because of our open policy and become a battering ram used against our socialist modernization programme. If you read some of the comment that have been made by people in Hong Kong and by bourgeois scholars in foreign countries, you will see that most of them insist that we should liberalize, or say that there are no human rights in China. These commentators oppose the very things we believe in and hope that we will change. But we shall continue to raise problems and solve them in the light of the realities in China.[8]

Deng later complained that these particular remarks had 'had no great effect' and that they not been disseminated throughout the Party.

On 2 September 1986 when Deng was prodded by the US TV correspondent Mike Wallace as to the real meaning of 'to get rich is glorious', Deng was testy in his complaint that people forget that the 'four modernizations' are 'socialist modernizations'. He then attempted to give Wallace a short lesson on the leftist mistakes of the Cultural Revolution. He placed the issue of getting rich within the context of leftist claims that 'poor communism was preferable to rich capitalism'.

> ...what we mean be getting rich is different from what you mean. Wealth in a socialist society means prosperity for the entire people. The principles of socialism are: first, development of production and second, common prosperity We permit some people and some regions to become prosperous first, for the purpose of achieving common prosperity faster. This is why our policy will not lead to polarization, to a situation where the rich get richer while the poor get poorer. To be frank, we shall not permit the emergence of a new bourgeoisie.[9]

In the contemporary contest such words now seem eerie, if not less than convincing as Hu Jintao seeks to address directly related problems of social justice.

In October 1986, however, a survey of 8,000 Beijing youth, gave Deng 87.5 per cent 'strong support'. The survey results did not anticipate the sudden spread in November and December of extraordinary student demonstrations. The latter revealed the deep contradictions, pent-up social frustrations and political confusion that had followed upon Deng's unprecedented reforms.

Deng turned on the Party Secretary General, Hu Yaobang, a close colleague who had been instrumental in setting up the agenda of economic reform and open door, for failing to arrest the spread of bourgeois liberation. Deng was profoundly disappointed that some in his Party had not taken a clear-cut stand on the difference between right and wrong and that bourgeois liberalization was festering inside the Party, itself. Subsequent to Hu Yaobang's dismissal, Deng told the Party on 30 December 1986:

'This is not a problem that has arisen in just one or two places, or just in the last couple of years; it is the result of the failure over the past several years to take a firm, clear-cut stand against bourgeois liberalization....' He also made it quite clear that the fight against bourgeois liberalization had to take place regardless of foreign opinion: 'We should not be afraid that people abroad will say we are damaging our reputation. We must take our own road and build a socialism adapted to conditions in China – that is the only way China can have a future.'[10]

Deng had invested a great deal of his own leadership in the consolidation of his reform as against any attempt by the left to revert back to the issues of the Cultural Revolution, when the issue of 'bourgeois liberalization' seized centre stage in Chinese politics in 1986. Bourgeois liberalization would not leave Deng Xiaoping alone and in the spring of 1989 the ensuing issue threatened to topple the Party's leadership.

Deng had started out with good intentions. He wanted to get rid of the 'spirit of the leader' and to institute a new process of institutionalization that included the growing reference to a socialist rule of law. In 1986 Deng acted like Mao, the 'Great Helmsman' (*da duoshou*) when he dismissed Hu Yaobang. Then in 1989 he did it again, dismissing Hu's successor, Zhao Ziyang, for the same lack of due vigilance in addressing bourgeois liberalization. The highest formal official in the Party was dismissed by veterans who rallied to the informal authority of Deng Xiaoping.

Arguably most student demonstrators wanted enhanced reform rather than regime change, but the dynamics of CCP leadership interaction with student leaders was problematic especially as some of the more radical students claimed parity or equality in negotiating with the Party leaders and their student organization attempted to consolidate itself outside the conventional parameters of Party control over student mass organization. Student dissidents like Wuer Kaixi challenged the Party's 'democratic centralism'. Zhao failed to convince the Politburo that student criticism was well-intended mass criticism rather than counterrevolutionary sentiment. Such criticism apparently revealed problems that did need to be addressed. Deng had done the most of any leader to bury 'class struggle as the key link'; however, the demonstrations, he said, represented counterrevolutionary 'turmoil'.

Deng very quickly moved to take back the reins of leadership and policy. He led the charge against bourgeois liberalization, but he also moved to counter leftists who wanted to use the 'turmoil' as an excuse to reinvigorate large-scale class struggle and stay the course of reform. Deng told the military brass in Beijing on 9 June 1989:

> Some comrades do not understand the nature of the problem [that is the confrontation between the four cardinal principles and 'bourgeois liber-alization']. They think it is simply a question of how to treat the masses. Actually, what we face is not simply ordinary people who are unable to distinguish between right and wrong. We also face a rebellious clique and a large number of dregs of society, who want to topple our country and overthrow our party.... I believe that after serious work, we can win the support of the overwhelming majority of our comrades within the Party concerning the nature of the incident and its handling.[11]

Deng conceded that the situation was very difficult to comprehend, and, therefore, a lot of good people were taken in by bad people. Deng had made the argument for institutionalization. He had declared that his own leadership was unimportant as his policies would be carried through time by the Party collectively. Now he argued that the complicated situation justified Party veterans who were experienced in dealing with complex twists and turns in seizing control of the duly constituted Party leadership of Zhao Ziyang. After so much reform, the 'spirit of the leader' was not yet dead.

On the one hand, Deng and his supporters wanted to ensure that the 'overwhelming majority' would come to realize the distinction between right and wrong. On the other, they had to deal with the immediate threat of a rollback to the Cultural Revolution. Deng needed to pre-empt any political linkage between counterrevolu-tion in the Square and the 'theory of productive forces'. Deng made a series of related statements on 9 June 1989. Claiming that there would be no change in 'basic principles and policies', Deng indicated that '...we must never turn China back into a country that keeps its doors closed'.[12] But at the same time he reiterated: 'In the reform of the political structure, one thing is certain: we must adhere to the system of the people's congresses instead of practicing the separation of the judicial, executive and legislative powers on the American pattern.'[13]

At the Fourth Plenary Session of the 13th Central Committee, on 23–24 June 1989, Deng's 9 June speech was turned into a programmatic statement. It was reaffirmed that Zhao had taken 'a passive approach to the adherence to the four cardinal principles and opposition to bourgeois liberalization'. Zhao's leadership in a nutshell was that 'he did something beneficial to the reform, the opening of China to the world', but that he 'gravely neglected party building', and 'supported the turmoil and split the Party'.

Deng's position was decisive as it was complex. He pre-empted the left by attacking Zhao, thus preventing a rollback to Cultural Revolutionary class struggle. At the same time, he protected his economic reform and the open door policies. These came with problems or contradictions, but these had to be solved so as to further enhance the living standards of the Chinese people. Deng took advantage of the opportunity of the Beijing Asian Games in 1990 to showcase the Chinese nation to the outside world, and during the 1990 visit of Lee Kuan Yew, both Jiang Zemin and Yang Shangkun emphasized that China would 'step up the process of reform and opening'.

Deng's 'Southern Tour' and the 'Socialist Market'

Deng in the 1989 crisis focused on bourgeois liberalization. On his programmatic statement of 9 June 1989, he protected his politics of economic reform and the open door. Interestingly, at that particular time he told his martial law generals that '...we must continue to combine economic planning with regulation by market forces. This should never be changed.'

The crisis passed and Deng returned to his great experiment. Most importantly, he changed his mind moving beyond the mid-1980s strategy of combining the market with the plan based on the predominance of public ownership and the ideological commitment to common prosperity. The change was orchestrated in his investigation tours to the special economic zones. A Chinese musical later celebrated this under the title, 'The Road to the Special Economic Zones'. Deng's 'socialism with Chinese characteristics' was much more than a road movie. Media coverage of his tours played up his great wisdom and ability to see far into the future. Deng used the media to create a political opinion in favour of accelerated reform.

Over the rearguard objections of 'leftists', Deng politically forced the pace of economic reform moving into a new higher stage of economic reform emphasizing structural changes to the state and the economy. His inspection tours to Wuhan, Guangzhou, Shenzhen, Zhuhai and Shanghai acquired great ideological significance and laid the groundwork for a policy leap at the 14 October 1992 Party Congress.

The 'Liberation of Productive Forces'

During the Cultural Revolution Deng had been accused of 'economism' and a 'theory of productive forces'. A question mark has hung over his head ever since as to whether his leadership and theory has moved China away from socialism to capitalism. Deng claimed that in the past the Chinese revolution served to 'emancipate' or 'liberate' (*jiefang*) the productive forces of the Chinese people from the control of 'imperialism, feudalism and bureaucrat-capitalism'. Once the socialist system was established the focus was on the creation of an economic structure that would secure the 'development of productive forces'. The way forward in 1992, however, called for a more vigorous 'liberation of productive forces' as 'reform' became 'revolution'. Deng laid out his theory: 'In the past, we only stressed the expansion of the productive forces under socialism, without mentioning the need to liberate them through reform. That conception was incomplete. Both the liberation and the expansion of the productive forces are essential.'[14]

When Mao opposed Party leaders for failing to move ahead with collectivization he accused them of acting like 'women with bound feet'. Now Deng said the same of those who would not liberate the productive forces.[15] Their fear of the spread of capitalism was so great that they could not liberate their minds.

Conventional Marxist-Leninist analysis had made the distinction between capitalism and socialism contingent upon the basic distinctions between ownership and distribution systems; for example, socialism, introduced 'each according to his work'. Under this principle labour was no longer a miserable commodity. Deng's idea of liberation now included a change in the position of the market vis-à-vis the plan. He stated:

> The proportion of planning to market forces is not the essential difference between socialism and capitalism. A planned economy is not equivalent to socialism, because there is planning under capitalism too; a market economy is not capitalism, because there are markets under socialism too. Planning and market forces are both means of controlling economic activity.[16]

Essentially, Deng decoupled the market from 'class'. Introducing the market under the rule of the CCP was akin to making a politically innocuous change to the organization of social technology.

Deng's Southern Tour theory represented the ideological highpoint in Deng's leadership of reform. It provided the underlying basis for the 14 November 1993 CCP Central Committee Decision on the Establishment of a Socialist Market Economic Structure as well as for subsequent amendment to Article 15 of the State Constitution that carried working to the effect: 'The State has put into practice a socialist market economy.' Deng endorsed the market not as supplementary, but as the fundamental means of resource allocation. He claimed that this was perfectly safe as public ownership still served as the 'mainstay' throughout the national economy. The 1993 Decision claimed the market for 'socialism': 'The socialist market economic structure is linked with the basic system of socialism. The establishment of this structure aims at enabling the market to play *the fundamental role in resource allocations under macro-economic control by the state.*'[17]

The introduction of notions such as the market and 'to get rich is glorious' was hardly apolitical. Deng had all along stressed that his advocacy of experiment and liberation was to support the needs of the people. If some people or regions should get rich first, this wealth was to support a future pattern of 'common prosperity'. The latter would not occur all at once. In fact it was postponed to a time when the productive forces would become more powerful. Deng had commented to leading Central Committee members on 24 December 1990 before the Southern Tour:

> Since the very beginning of the reform we have been emphasizing the need for seeking common prosperity; that would surely be the central issue some day. Socialism does not mean allowing a few people to grow rich while the overwhelming majority live in poverty. No, that's not socialism. The greatest superiority of socialism is that it enables all the people to prosper, and command prosperity is the essence of socialism.[18]

In Deng's brave new experimental world, efficiency was linked to competition. In fact the 1993 Decision on the market referenced the slogan, 'efficiency is primary and fairness is supplementary' (*xiaoyi wei zhu, gongzheng weifu*). The Decision also repeated leadership reference to 'three favourable directions' (*sange youli yu*) that included the liberation of productive forces with admonitions to ensure against polarization and to support common prosperity.

Policy concerning the society and economy underwent profound change. The introduction of the market did lead to changes in basic structure. As the planned economy was dismantled there was a political call for a rational legal culture that would support an updated 'moral division of labour between the state, related "mass", or popular social associations, schools and public agents, families and individuals for authenticating rights in the practical transactions of society'.[19] The move to market meant a reduction in state provision of services generally and a search for new formats of partnership in society based, for example, on the Hainan model of 'small government, big society' (*xiao zhengfu, da shehui*) to provide new services, hence the logic in the original 14 November 1993 Decision:

It is necessary to establish an income distribution system which takes the principle of 'to each according to his work' as its mainstay, gives priority to efficiency while taking fairness into account so as to encourage some localities and people to become prosperous first while adhering to the road to common prosperity. It is also necessary to establish a multi-layered social security system and provide both urban and rural people with a degree of security commensurate to china's reality so as to promote economic development and social stability. All these major links comprise an organic entity, interrelated and mutually conditioning, together forming the basic framework of the socialist market economy. It is necessary to establish a legal system in line with and corresponding to these major links and to adopt down-to-earth measures to push the overall reform forward actively step by step and promote the development of the social productive forces.[20]

The same Decision had implications for the system of distribution, as it called for the introduction of 'competitive mechanisms for rewarding individual labor and to break away from egalitarianism, so as to implement the principle of more pay for more work'. It was acknowledged that the Decision would likely result in a certain widening of the 'income gap'. The extent to which the old system of support was to be dismantled was suggested in the Decision's following requirement: 'The support of the agenda in rural areas will be shouldered chiefly by their families and supplemented by community assistance.'

The Political Economy of 'Newly Emerging Interests'

Reform sanctioned a new pattern of competition in the economy and encouraged the development of 'newly emerging interests' in society. While it was one thing to suggest that some could get rich first, what happens to those who were not in a position to compete and who must wait for common prosperity? What would the Party do about the related contradictions in society?

The answer incorporated Deng's strategy for institutionalization. Jiang Zemin, the new Party General Secretary, addressed this concern at a financial study class for leading cadres. He urged correct analysis of conflicts among the people. Such analysis had to start with the recognition of the complicated and diverse nature of such conflict particularly as the market economy had not fully well developed and the forms of ownership and distribution had become somewhat 'pluralized' in the uneven conditions of the 'primary stage of socialism':

> When problems of bureaucracy and corruption among leading cadres are seriously jeopardizing people's interests, if socialist democracy and the legal system are not far from perfect and people cannot resort to democratic and legal means to effectively stop these problems, conflicts of interests among the people may turn into violent clashes of interests.... They can only be resolved through the socialist system, the use of economic means, ideological and political work, democracy and the legal system and the readjustment and harmony of interests. In a socialist market economy, it is necessary...to properly handle the interests between individuals, the collective and the state and properly handle the interests of interest subjects of different economic sectors, establish diverse distribution systems on the basis of the coexistence of diverse ownership systems, establish and improve a national macroeconomic regulation mechanism and a social security system, and fully make use of the market mechanism to distribute and regulate the interests of different quarters. This calls for further development of the legal system and expanding the scope of political involvement by various social strata.[21]

The rule of law in this new context became part of the utilitarian purpose of the CCP to ensure stability through the 'adjustment of interests'. Also, Jiang kept right on with the theme of liberation. He consolidated a basic change to the principle of distribution. He outlined the following position at the 15th Party Congress:

> We shall keep to the system in which distribution according to work is primary and in which a variety of modes of distribution co-exist. By combining remuneration according to work and remuneration according to factors of production put in, and by giving priority to efficiency with due consideration to equity, such a system is conducive to optimizing the allocation of resources, promoting economic development and maintaining social stability.[22]

In other words, diversity in the system of distribution was to be tolerated and even encouraged in so far as it did basically challenge the primacy of 'each according to his/her own work'.

Deng's death on 12 September 1997 was an extraordinary moment in time. Foreign observers were concerned as to the course of reform under what they thought was a bland ideologue who had never managed to come out from under Deng's shadow.

Politically Jiang wisely opted for a proven political strategy. He inherited Deng's consensus for reform. In his October 1997 political report, 'Hold High the Great Banner of Deng Xiaoping Theory for an All-round Advancement of the Cause of Building Socialism with Chinese Characteristics into the 21st Century',[23] Jiang was totally self-effacing. He just ladled out the rhetorical continuity of theory and praxis, heaping praise on 'Deng Xiaoping Theory' as it promotes 'socialism with Chinese characteristics'.

Jiang eulogized the centrality of praxis and reaffirmed the need to maintain primary vigilance against the 'left' as opposed to the 'right'. He recounted how Deng's theory rejected Hua Guofeng's 'two whatevers' and constituted the correct 'continuation and development of Mao Zedong Thought'. Deng had upheld the leadership of the 'first generation' of Mao and Zhou; he had inherited their wisdom, but at the same time, using their 'seeking the truth from the facts', he broke with 'outmoded conventions on the basis of new practice' so that he could enter 'a new realm of Marxism'.[24] Jiang continued Deng's great experiment.

Jiang took the final step in a highly symbolic political act of confirming new Party line on reform through amending the State Constitution in March 1999. Article 12 originally mentioned the initial stage of socialism, but the revised wording stated: 'Our country will remain in the initial stage of socialism *for a long time to come.*'[25] The same article also included new reference to the steady improvement of socialist institutions and 'the development of a new socialist market economy'. New wording in Article 14 confirmed the qualified establishment of plural forms of ownership and distribution:

In the initial stage of socialism, the country shall uphold the basic economic system in which public ownership is dominant and *diverse forms of ownership develop side by side*, and it shall uphold the distribution system with distribution according to work remaining dominant and a variety of modes of distribution coexisting.[26]

While under Jiang the Party continued to adhere to a strategy of change within continuity, it has faced very interesting times. Social structures and economic relationships have become much more complicated. The Party no longer has the same capacity to network through society and the complexity of society has required new ways of thinking about the division of political labour and the practice of governance. This serves as the basic background to Jiang's introduction of the concept of the 'three represents' (*sange daibiao*).

Jiang hoped to fashion an effective political response to the structural changes in society. He called upon the Party to represent the 'development trend of China's advanced productive forces, the orientation of China's advanced culture, and the fundamental interests of the overwhelming majority of the Chinese people'.[27]

This builds upon Dengist Southern Tour theory that called for both the 'liberation' and 'development of productive forces'. However, the consequent changes in social and economic structure opened up new spaces where there was a significant absence of functioning Party organization. Jiang asked the question: How does the Party recruit and consolidate itself organizationally in such circumstances?

Deng started something when at the inception of reform he decided that the intellectuals could become part of proletariat and thus were placed out of the reach of class struggle. Jiang went further by inviting the entrepreneurs to take out Party membership. In so far as the left was concerned, this was an ideological bombshell, but from Jiang's political point of view, the Party needed to find a way to extend Party leadership into the new areas in society and the economy that had opened up under reform. This was not a matter of concession to the bourgeoisie as it was a politically appropriate united front task of cooperation and cooptation.

Jiang no longer had the option of class-based mass mobilization to deal with challenges to the life of the Party's 'socialist' regime. Alternatively, he provided new protection in law for 'newly emerging interests', but he also sought to find a way of coopting new material interests that might otherwise form their own independent political base. Shoring up the Party's 'ruling power' in such circumstances was necessarily complex.

The country's workforce had become much diversified and mobile. Jiang noted in 2000 that a 130 million workforce was located in 1.5 million private enterprises and 31 million individual households. These new categories included entrepreneurs and technical personnel in private scientific and technical enterprise, managerial and technical staff employed by foreign-funded enterprises, and self-employed private entrepreneurs. Such diversification made it more difficult to handle the relation between fairness and efficiency.

Jiang recognized the opening of new spaces within society and the economy wherein there was too little Party organization. He believed that one of the main political tasks of the Party was to organize new formats of leadership in both public and private enterprise and particularly to find ways to 'step up Party building among non-public economic organizations'. He conceded that there were no CCP members in 86 per cent of China's enterprises. In short, 'three represents' was his strategy for extending Party leadership throughout a changing society and economy.

Willy Wo-Lap Lam, in his analysis, suggests that Jiang was much more interested in cultivating the 'advanced productive forces' than looking after the interests of the 'overwhelming majority', but this might well be a false antithesis.[28] Jiang was worried about control in the private sector of the economy, but he was also very concerned about maintaining Party rule through responding to the 'feelings of the people'. Although there may have been tension between Jiang and his successor, Hu Jintao, the latter sustained the focus on the 'three represents' for the same good political reasons, and some elements of Hu's concept of 'harmony' hark back to Jiang's view on Party rule.

Jiang's opinion on how to go about the three represents accords with the contemporary emphasis on a 'scientific' approach to governance as the rational and informed management of public affairs. Jiang told the Party:

> If our party is to meet all the requirements of the 'three represents' we have got to be able to grasp their practice and provide leadership to them and always march in the vanguard of socio-economic development.... This means that we should know how to obtain convincing first-hand information by grasping the problems and getting a clear idea about what is going on, derive the norms from such information by refining and summarizing in a scientific way, and use the norms to guide our work.[29]

Whether or not Jiang was too wordy and bland is quite beside the point. He perpetuated Dengist reform on the successful basis of change within continuity that featured 'seeking the facts from the truth'. He turned out to be a survivor in an extremely complex and sometimes utterly unpredictable context. Compare Jiang with Hu Yaobang and Zhao Ziyang. They revved up the market's motor and unleashed new forces in the economy, but they could not keep up with the political contradictions that translated into popular disaffection and mass demonstrations. Jiang consolidated the trend in the liberation of productive forces. Like Deng, he seemed to know when to move right and when to move left. He supported the 'rule of law' and acting according to law in state administration and then he turned around and suppressed the Falungong. At the same time he made common cause with Zhu Rongji to ensure China's entry into the WTO. Jiang with Deng's borrowed prestige established China's 'rise'. His was a highly successful political strategy predicated explicitly on change within continuity.

When Hu Jintao assumed the Party leadership he carefully rolled the 'three represents' into the strategy of change within continuity so that we now have a much elongated concept, Marxism-Leninism Mao Zedong Thought, the theory of Deng Xiaoping and the 'three represents'. Premature Western speculation that

Hu as a new generational leader would finally cut the Party's primal umbilical cord to depart from democratic centralism and to embrace more familiar notions of 'democracy' was just plain wrong. Hu's political experience had nothing to do with liberal democracy, and at least in hindsight it seems hardly appropriate to have jumped to such a conclusion that a CCP senior leader would turn his back on Party rule so as to satisfy foreign opinion at the expense of China's 'independence and self-reliance'.

Like Jiang, Hu Jintao has had to wrestle with the underlying question of Party authority in the context of accelerated reform and market relationships. Building on Jiang's 'three represents', he has responded with his own formal thinking on how to build political democracy in China in the context of a 'socialist market'. Also, while he laboured to reinforce the regime's established ideological base, he has taken considerable initiative with a correction of course. Deng's policies remain sacrosanct, but Hu has moved somewhat to the left in the Party's political spectrum, emphasizing the need for social justice and harmony in light of the divisions and cleavages that have affected China throughout the transition to the new marketplace. This was part of the new packaging of the governing Party responding to the feelings of the people and looking after the needs of the people, hence 'the people first'. Deng Xiaoping, himself, had predicted that the issues of polarization and common prosperity would become key issues in the future.

Hu Jintao at the Fourth Plenary Session of the 16th CCP Central Committee reflected on the original issue concerning some getting rich first. He obviously wanted to bring the Party State back into the economy and to review the relation of market to state guidance.

> Correctly handle the relationship between having distribution according to labour as the mainstay and practicing a variety of distribution methods, encourage some regions and people to get rich ahead of others, pay attention to social fairness, rationally readjust the income distribution pattern, earnestly adopt effective measures to resolve problems of excessive income disparities between regions and between some members of society

and gradually achieve common affluence of all the people. Correctly handle the relationship between market mechanism and macro regulation and control, persist in acting according to market economy rules, give greater play to the basic role of the market in resource distribution, strengthen and improve state macro regulation and control and promote the highly vigorous and efficient and healthy operation of the national economy.[30]

At the same time Hu has revealed a penchant for comment on national history and he has moved in a somewhat populist direction, particularly in his focus on rural China and the need to repair the Party's base of support in the countryside. His ideological focus on 'harmony' contrasts with Cultural Revolutionary focus on 'class struggle as the key link', but he stresses 'harmony' in light of the need to address the contradictions of fast growth. Perhaps, paradoxically, his stress on harmony has invoked a new interest in Confucian values in society. In the past, ideology was largely concerned with the ways in which Confucianism had reinforced social inequality, but history is now being used in support of the CCP's nationalist credentials and to undo some of the damage generated in the earlier rush to market.

The Hu Jintao Leadership and the Private Property Issue

Having Deng Xiaoping in the wings and having Jiang Zemin in the wings may not be quite the same thing. However, Hu's career had demonstrated a similar deference to authority and the principle of ideological continuity, involving the ideological canonization of past leadership. Hu carefully played the necessary political game. He inducted Jiang into the Party pantheon that included Mao and Deng, and initially he took a low profile for himself. In 2004–05, however, the outlines of his leadership started to take shape. Like Jiang, Hu appears to be very concerned about the loss of a moral centre in Chinese society. Also like Jiang, he has to face a more complex society and he has been seeking to develop new strategies to ensure Party rule, especially in the context of mounting contradictions within China's system of ownership.

His correction involved paying more attention to public feeling and identifying the Party more emphatically with social justice, particularly in the countryside where many had realized the same gains as their city counterparts. Hu's regime reduced the tax burdens of the countryside. The original social contract – perennial fast growth in return for acceptance of continued Party rule – has been somewhat adjusted to take into account a stronger emphasis on social injustice.

Hu's leadership, however, attempted to cut its teeth on one outstanding issue that goes to the heart of the issue of 'socialism' versus 'capitalism'. Hu took up the issue of private property. On the one hand, there was a desire to ensure against cadre corruption that had siphoned off publicly owned assets for private purpose during the reform of state enterprise. On the other, and most importantly, he needed to reassure the peasants in the countryside that the reform's requirements would continue on into the future. In particular the Party needed to protect and develop the peasant's 'right of use' (*shiyong quan*), of publicly owned means of production.

Early in his leadership Hu seemed to run into a brick wall when he suggested changing the State Constitution to give new recognition to private property. This proposition was ideological dynamite for conservatives who feared the rout of Chinese socialism. Demonstrating reserves of political fortitude, he withdrew from NPC legislation waiting to build up his political strength, and then successfully reintroduced the revision that passed in March 2004. The following state constitutional amendment represents a key wording in modern Chinese history since 1949: 'The lawful private property of citizens shall not be encroached upon' (*gongminde hefade siyou caichan bushou qinfan*).

Marxist-Leninists are in theory supposed to 'smash' the capitalist state and to abolish private property and see the transition to complete public ownership of the means of production. Chinese civil law is rooted in Soviet and European tradition. The Soviet reinforced Continental tradition preferred the 'totality of ownership'.[31] This was politically congenial because it gave the state priority in the public ownership including wholly state-owned property in the cities or collectively owned land in the countryside.

The original preference for 'ownership' as distinct from 'property rights' (*caichan quan*) reflected the revolutionary regime's desire to achieve the greatest control over the means of production. Ownership rights (*suoyou quan*) assume unqualified and comprehensive ownership. The Anglo-American concept of 'property rights' is more flexible in that allows a plural involvement in property ownership. Chinese reform mainly wanted to fraction rights, and in particular to provide the right of use to peasants so as to encourage production increases while avoiding compromising the state's ultimate ownership rights. Presumably the latter was needed to maintain China's 'socialist' credentials.

The CCP has wanted flexibility in reform, but it has also been very keen to protect the pre-eminence of public ownership. The right to own land in the cities is a matter of form that is politically important particularly in the contentious context of the state's appropriation of land for public purpose. However, for those involved in property relations in the cities, the right of use has been critical.

There is, however, a deeply paradoxical aspect to the situation of ownership rights in China. In the context of reform most of the country has been involved in an ownership experiment as the leaders 'grope stones on the bottom of the river bed'. Practice in terms of the rights of the state, collectives and individuals has often been determined in political and economic praxis without *a priori* reference to the law, the underlying jurisprudential principles of ownership which are inflexible. Perhaps the most confusing aspect is the problem of post-Commune ownership by administrative and natural villages in the countryside that have had to deal with the consequences of the household contract system. In the reform period there is a spectacular gap between substance and form or theory and practice. Property relations have been the subject of deliberate experiment in reform China.

Market reform came with a strongly qualified pluralization of both distribution and ownership systems. Joint ventures with foreigners were created and in some cases foreigners could wholly own enterprise. A whole new generation of private entrepreneurs was created in this reform context and there was mounting demand for the protection of their property rights against corrupt officials while in the countryside households that obtained the 'right of use' of land wanted to be sure of their future position regarding these rights.

Even before the decision to introduce the market as the fundamental basis of distribution, an amendment was passed in the NPC on 12 April 1988 that attempted to enhance the status of private ownership while at the same time clearly emphasizing the pre-eminence of the state in the control of all property. The latter was no longer a supplementary matter but an important component of the national economy, hence the revised Article 11 indicated:

> The state permits the private sector of the economy to exist and develop within the limits prescribed by law. The private sector of the economy is a complement to the socialist public economy. The state protects the lawful rights and interests of the private sector of the economy, and exercises guidance, supervision and control over the private sector of the economy.[32]

Such an amendment provided some sort of encouraging political signal, but the protection of private property remained a politically pressing problem in practice. The demand for protection focused on getting equal treatment in law of private and public property, and this was the key issue in 2004 and 2008.

In 2004 private property received unprecedented, but still carefully guarded, state constitutional reference. Private property was still in a precarious political and legal position especially when compared to the generous protection of public property. The legal system was both designed to facilitate and predisposed to protect the latter, but not the former. Politically, public ownership was supposed to stand as a guarantee of Deng's great experiment. However, the weakness of private property had encouraged official corruption. Those with private property were especially exposed to official demands for fees and prerequisites. Some tried to avoid this exposure by hiding under a 'red hat' (*hong mao*) as they posed as collective enterprise in the hopes of escaping more excessive demands of rent-seeking officials. Also at the time of passage, reformers emphasized that the new law on property would strengthen households' claims to the means of production in the countryside.

It is very hard, however, to make sense of the contemporary Chinese understanding of ownership and property relations. It took an extraordinary seven rounds of discussion before the new March 2007 property law was passed in China.[33] The issue had been festering politically since the 1980s and the development of private ownership and the latter's lack of protection as compared to private property.

The media coverage of a jointly-signed letter by leftists opposed to the 2007 property law gives an interior glimpse into the related politics. Professor Lin Dong of the Central Party School explained in an interview that at first the central authorities were content to regard the letter as a legitimate part of public debate. She revealed that Professor Gong Xiantian, Peking University, claimed that the proposed law's equal protection of private and public property was unconstitutional as it conflicted with the Constitution's wording and related wording in the civil code that 'socialist public property is sacred and inviolable'.

Gong had argued that such a law would create an imbalance between the rich and poor and contribute to significant polarization, and the continued enjoyment of illegally acquired state assets. Lin had originally helped to vet the letter at the end of 2005, but she noted a basic change in the attitude of the central authorities:

Wu Bangguo, Chairman of the NPC SC, personally instructed the NPC to suspend its legislation and solicited Gong Xiantian's opinions face to face. However, the central authorities later discovered that something was wrong with the motive of the opposition raised by this scholar, as behind its back, the opposition was not really aimed at the draft law, but at the general policy of reform and opening up, and at the reform line initiated by Deng Xiaoping. Hence the NPC has decided not to take heed.[34]

There was a basic change in the status of the letter. It had gone from a legitimate expression of informed NPC debate to an oppositional instance of conspiracy against the state.

Some authors such as Peter Ho are inclined to argue that the political leadership is involved in deliberate ambiguity to avoid extremely serious and sensitive issues in society. In a 2001 *China Quarterly* publication, Peter Ho noted the problem of unclear property structure in the rural areas was a matter of 'deliberate institutional ambiguity':

> ...institutional indeterminancy is the 'lubricant' on which the system runs: the ambiguity of the legal rules allows the land tenure system to function at the current stage of economic reform. Moreover, this institutional indeterminancy is partly the result of efforts by the central leadership to create leeway for reacting to societal developments. For this reason, I speak of 'deliberate institutional ambiguity' as upheld by the state.[35]

This might suggest that the wish for the rule of law's clarity is operative only some of the time. One wonders how it can be possible to enter into all sorts of new complex contractual agreements without abundant clarity as to who actually owns what and how the regime can even survive the outraged feelings of the people when it comes to failure to protect their property. As Yongshun Cai indicates, for example, social stability is the number one priority of the regime; hence he notes:

> The resistance of the weak is effective when it becomes so widespread that it threatens social stability. Under these circumstances, the Chinese government has an incentive 'to get the struggles off the streets and into the courts' or to 'make the revolution before the people do'.[36]

Property Law of the PRC

The March 2007 property law focused on the regulation of property relationships and 'the use of things' that would obviate disputes and promote China's national economy and 'socialist harmonious society' on the basis of a 'scientific development concept'. The private sector had grown by leaps and bounds without the benefit of transparent legal title. The new law was to further the developing conception of equal public and private property rights. Wang Jiafu, CASS Institute of Law, put it this way: 'A market economy requires that market players enjoy the same rights, follow the same rules and bear the same responsibility. We are not able to engage in the market economy it they are not equal.'[37] To deal with the 'opposition' it was reiterated that the law would ensure that all state-owned property would receive protection under the law. NPC members noted that 200,000 hectares of rural land had been taken from farmers annually for industrial purposes and that more that 65 per cent of 'massive incidents', or petitions and protests involving a large group of people in rural areas was related to land expropriations. NPC member Yao hailed the law's purpose: 'Such regulations will provide farmers a powerful lever to safeguard their rights and interests when they have to give up their land.'[38]

The new law was touted as part of the Hu administration's reforms for greater social justice. The law was, for example, hailed for its protection of all the beneficiaries of housing system reform whose 'rights and interests' included ownership of their own homes. Their divided shares of the title of a building were affirmed as an important right within the ownership of private immovable property.

Critical American observers are not satisfied with the new law as it does not go far enough in confirming private property as the primary feature of the state and its economy. While welcoming new protection for private property, James Dorn, of the CATO Institute, indicated at the related roundtable of the Congressional Executive Commission on China that the issue is not equal protection, but pre-eminence of private property vis-à-vis other forms of property:

> Markets work best when property is fully protected by the rule of law and people are free to choose. We should not forget the words of James Madison, the chief architect of the US Constitution: 'The personal right to acquire property, which is a natural right, gives to property, when acquired, a right to protection as a social right.' China is beginning to recognize the right to private property, but only as a right bestowed by the state not as

a natural (inalienable) right. Consequently, private property can never be secure until there is a fundamental revolution in political philosophy that places the individual, not the state, at the center of the moral universe and limits to the power of government.[39]

CCP analysis is correct in its assumption that American 'bourgeois' experts want to change China's 'colour'.

The rule of law may have been hailed across the land and Hu has since made it part of his 'scientific development concept', but when it comes to clarifying property rights the CCP appears to have opted for an opportune ambiguity in a vital area of society and the economy. However, some element of clarification of property relations was found to be politically necessary in regard to pressing political issues. Private property has undergone very significant expansion. Moreover, some of the thorniest issues of property relations pertained to the confusion of private and collective property. Ho may be right, at least in part, in his emphasis on deliberate ambiguity.

Wang Zhaoguo, as Vice Chairman of the NPC Standing Committee, offered some insight on this in his explanation to fellow SC members. He insisted that the drafters were right in their assumption that it was necessary 'to leave some room for deepening the reform in future'. On the critical issue of lifting restrictions on the transfer and mortgage of the right to land in the rural collective context, he stated:

> On the question whether restrictions on the transfer and mortgage of the right to land, contractual management and the house-site-use right can be lifted. In view of the fact that at present, the social security system in the rural areas of our country has not yet been established in an all-round way and that the right to land contractual management and house-site use right provide the peasants lifelong foundation, the conditions for lifting such restrictions are not yet right, when considered from the perspective of the country as a whole. In order to maintain the laws currently in force and the policies of the State on rural land at this present stage, as well as to leave some room for revising relevant laws or adjusting relevant policies in the future, the draft property law stipulates, 'persons enjoying the right to land contractual management shall be entitled to circulate such right by adopting

such means as subcontract, exchange and assignment in accordance with the provision in the law on Land Contract in Rural Areas'.[40]

The Politics of Housing Reform

In practice, throughout the 1990s and up to the present, there has been enormous change in the spreading ownership of housing in the cities. Homeowners' Associations of various organizational nature have been springing up in the major cities, often to protect homeowners from developer encroachment and official malfeasance. In the urban setting more than 70 per cent of urban households own their own homes. That may be the good news, but the bad news is that the state still jealously holds on to its prerogatives of ownership and the state capacity for expropriation is extraordinary. Before the early 1990s those who were expropriated were compensated with new homes, often in their original neighbourhoods, but local government recoiled at the escalating expense and preferred unilaterally to compensate those expropriated with inadequate cash payments based on unfair evaluation that pushed a lot of people out of their original highly desirable neighbourhoods in the city core.

The new guarantee of land use for up to 70 years can still be quickly and arbitrarily terminated if it is deemed 'in the public interest'. The latter rationale has often been unfairly interpreted to include for business purposes. Unpalatable corruption enters this picture with deals struck between developers and officials. According to Yongshun Cai, 80 per cent of the housing demolition is really carried out for business purposes rather than for the public interest.[41] The Supreme People's Court and the State Council have been looking for remedial means to ensure proper compensation; in the meantime there is growing political angst that was, for example, featured in the national media during the approval of the new property law, itself.

The Case of Yang Wu's House

In the Yang Wu case in Chongqing City, the developer had a court order for demolition and municipal party and departmental personnel were on side. Yang's house became the most widely circulated photo among mainland citizens. The protection of the new law was not at issue as the latter did not come into effect until 1 October. After two years of bitter argument with the developers, Yang's single house still stood at the centre of a construction site in downtown Chongqing. (The other 280 households had already left.) Yang defiantly stood his ground. From the rooftop of his house he waved the national flag and unfurled his banner, 'A citizen's legitimate private property cannot be violated.' He stored at his home liquefied petroleum gas, distilled water and boarding materials to protect his property.[42]

The media reports presented conflicted facts. One daily claimed that he wanted 20 million yuan (US $2.56 million) but his wife counterclaimed on television that they only wanted the same sized apartment in the original location. Wang Wei, Manager of the Development Department, told the newspapers: 'We've now invested 300 million yuan (US $38.79 million) into the project. We will suffer huge losses if this matter remains deadlocked.' Wu's wife required the protection of the Constitution and the new property law indicating a very familiar point that the new shopping centre was not a matter of 'public interest', but a business move by a developer.

Jiang Ping, a senior law authority at the China University of Political Science and Law and a member of the team that drafted the Property Law of the PRC, intervened with a less than encouraging commentary on her layman's view of the law: 'She is not in a position to judge what is or isn't in the public interest. If the compensation is legal and reasonable, they should move out; if they don't think so, they may file lawsuits and take this issue to court.'[43]

The Hong Kong *Ming Pao* reported on the related local politics: 'As a result of the high degree of concern expressed by the public, the Chongqing municipal party committee and government have reportedly felt the pressure and convened meetings to deliberate on a solution, fearing that an improper handling of the incident will cause the public to react vigorously, to the detriment of Chongqing's image.'[44]

The current envelope of reform appears to include a focus on extending 'right of use' in countryside so as to enhance the peasant sense of security and to create the same kind of flexibility as already exists in the cities. This extension will, however, once again raise the ideological issue as to whether private property is being advanced at the expense of the socialist principle of public ownership. The status of private property is a key to the political distinction between 'socialism' and 'capitalism'. And the latter is necessary to the distinction between 'capitalist democracy' and 'socialist democracy'. While the Party has responded to the 'rights and interests' of newly emerging interests; it has focused on the 'overwhelming majority of the people'. This obviates the need to rely on a new middle class as is the case in liberal democracy.

The transition to market was a brilliant idea based on an incredible experiment. It is hard to know whether China's leaders gave careful thought to all of the implications of the market as they 'groped for rocks on the river bed'. The suggestion that the market's introduction is just a matter of social technical change was never that reassuring.

Considering the enormity of the consequent social and economic change in China's political economy, the Party strategy of 'deliberate institutional ambiguity' plus 'acting according to law', while contradictory has been applied on different locations in different issue areas. Things are evolving on the basis of the *ad hoc* policy and organizational strategies of the 'governing Party' and still there is not only governance but extraordinary economic development. Common sense would argue, how is this possible without clear legal understanding of who owns what? The stakes for people in terms of their life opportunities are truly enormous and there is now in China a spreading 'righteous resistance' where the protesting people, or *laobaixing*, repeat the law and related policy back to the Party demanding that it live up to its state goals. Today's 'crying motley of contradictions' seems to be more aggravated, but then the Chinese economy is still backstopped by tremendous state capacity and the jury is still out on the question of whether Hu's correction of course will effectively address these contradictions.

Whether Hu Jintao's regime has the political capacity to make good on its stated goals is an open question, but at least the underlying issue has been well articulated. Hu has told the Party: 'We must always put the interests of the people first.' Deng had originally emphasized 'socialism is not poverty' in reaction to the costs to the people of the Cultural Revolution and its neglect of productive forces and material standards of living in favour of politically extreme class struggle and instability. Under Deng and Jiang, there was protestation against expected inequalities that attend the wholesale resort to the 'market'. On the one hand, there was an unusually strong emphasis on the primacy of the market as the 'fundamental mechanism' for distribution and this was reflected in the often stated principle, 'efficiency is primary and justice is supplementary'. There was at least some formal concern about growing gaps in the material standard of living as some did indeed 'get rich first'. In theory the latter was to contribute eventually to the wealth of society as a whole and Deng's 'three favourable directions' had called for 'common prosperity' as against 'polarization'.

Under Hu Jintao formal concern has become more emphatic in the explicit recognition that fast growth produced inequality and social disequilibria. In a major foray into dialectics, Hu Jintao in his bellwether speech to the Fourth Plenary Session of the 16th CCP Central Committee Fourth Plenum, 16th CCPCC directed the following:

> Correctly handle the relationship between having distribution according to labour as the mainstay and practicing a variety of distribution methods, encourage some regions and people to get rich ahead of others, pay attention to social fairness, rationally readjust the income distribution pattern, earnestly adopt effective measures to resolve problems of excessive income disparities between regions and between some members of society and gradually achieve common affluence of all the people. Correctly handle the relationship between market mechanism and macro regulation and control, persist in acting according to market economy rules, give greater play to the basic role of the market in resource distribution, strengthen

an improve state macro regulation and control and promote the highly vigorous and efficient and healthy operation of the national economy.[45]

Hu's emphasis on 'harmonious development' is a practical correction of course, if not a swing to the left. Political consensus has been built on the continuity of principle that cuts across the four generations of leaders. Hu has not said that Deng or Jiang were wrong, but he has moved to deal with the outstanding matter of social justice that originated with their rush to market. Moreover, Hu has extended Deng's post-1978 strategy of institutionalization placing even greater emphasis on the 'governing party's' scientific management of public affairs. Hu indicated in a 26 June 2005 speech:

> A harmonious society should feature democracy, the rule of law, equity, justice, sincerity and vitality. Such a society will give full scope to people's talent and creativity, enable all people to gain wealth. If the Party is to 'serve the people', then law and democracy in this scenario are institutions that will moderate social conflict and sustain unity and social justice.[46]

The ledger of reform under Hu is politically interesting. The Party controls the market; the market does not yet control the Party. Hu never intended a liberal democratic breakthrough, but in his attempt to achieve a 'harmonious society', he has endorsed the reform emphases on the rule of law, human rights and democracy, giving much more attention to 'democracy' as it relates to formats of consultation and participation. There is a controlled populism in his governance 'to serve the people', and 'placate public feeling'. Political reform is especially utilitarian. And 'democracy' is largely a matter of servicing socio-economic consequences of reform. According to the 2005 White Paper, 'democracy' is about respecting the overwhelming majority while protecting everyone's 'rights and interests'. The socio-cultural aspects of accelerated reform are continuously addressed within a conservative moral rhetoric and reference to the Party history of Chinese nationalism.

Hu's administration sees the national economy as an 'organic whole' and is reviewing the balance of macro-regulation and market forces. There is a disposition to achieve a greater degree of control over the negative outcomes of rapid economic expansion. Bank credit is likely to be more closely controlled, and at the same time the campaign against corruption fitfully continues. There is heightened political concern over the encroachment on rural arable land and need to improve conditions in rural areas so as to keep population in the hinterland and slow down urbanization. The floating population is especially vulnerable to changes in the domestic and international economy.

There is a growing political focus on 'harmonious society' in order to achieve more active state-led development and social justice. Much of these initiatives and supposedly new thinking draws from the CCP's own well of political and organizational experience, and the parameters of reform are still governed by a strategy of change within continuity that has supported the goal of 'socialism with Chinese characteristics' since December 1978.

5
CHINA'S NEW 'MODEL' OF INTERNATIONAL RELATIONS

The term 'model' here has to be used advisedly. If anything, the Chinese 'model' is an anti-model model. This connects with the story of the CCP as it has dealt with revolution and modernization. The emphasis has been on dialectical learning with modesty. While China's leaders have rediscovered China's 'ancient civilization', they have wisely declined to survey 'benignly the nations from [China's] heights'. 'Middle Kingdom-ism' as well as treaty port social Darwinism for the most part passed into history, whereas the post-1949 trend relating Marxist-Leninist principles with Chinese national praxis realistically emphasized the importance of national conditions both in terms of approach to development and in conducting relations with other states.

The lesson of containment as described in Chapter 2 was that China, in expanding its circles of mutual recognition, should not claim leadership. The success in undermining containment confirmed the need for low posture in dealing with international relations. Mao confronted the Soviet Union for its failure in the leadership of the world communist movement, but he did not then claim Chinese leadership of this movement. The five principles of peaceful coexistence transcended the requirements of proletarian internationalism, particularly as China normalized its relations with the US and the Soviet Union while still 'opposing hegemony'. And possibly picking up Zhou Enlai's view of the world, Deng Xiaoping later confirmed: '...we believe that there is not, and cannot be, any centre in the international communist movement'.[1] By not claiming leadership China concentrated squarely on its own opportunity for development.

Deng had repeatedly claimed that 'China would never seek hegemony'; and in crafting China's response to the international backlash against Tiananmen Square in 1989, Deng had reiterated to the Foreign Ministry that China must 'never claim leadership'.[2]

Notwithstanding the often repeated claim that China 'will never seek hegemony', contemporary Western 'realism' has tried to perpetuate inadequate Cold War assumptions about China's real motive for expansion as a new and militarily 'muscular' 'superpower'. 'Realism' originally focused attention on the interests of states in the context of anarchy, and the principle of self-help justified arms build-up and resort to war to protect states in this condition of anarchy.

The only part of this argument that has any connection with the Chinese is the reference to the importance of state sovereignty. Otherwise Chinese analysis has consistently opposed such 'realism' as dysfunctional in that it justified the balance of power based on the spread of alliance systems around the world at the expense of national self-determination and state sovereignty. The realist system of international politics was predicated in a hierarchical great power responsibility that essentially denied principles of equality and reciprocity in the state system. The depth of Chinese commitment to alternative emphasis on cooperation based upon equality and reciprocity is confirmed in diplomatic thinking and their approach to containment and the UN. Despite being 'contained', and despite Cold War alignments, Chinese foreign policy and diplomacy over time focused on the extension of China's relations with other states regardless of their ideological position.

The analysis in Chapter 2 points to a related history of widening circles of recognition and engagement and a continuing focus on development in foreign and domestic policy. This chapter will now turn to how this historical basis is now being used to develop an alternative reading and related 'model' of international relations. The key to this development, however, is the equation of this model, as advocated by China with the universalism of the UN and adaptation to the 'democratization of international relations' and 'diversity of civilizations' and win–win international economic cooperation.

The Contemporary Relevance of 'Harmony with Differences'

The Chinese approach to 'diversity of civilization' is directly linked to past operational strategy of Zhou Enlai, namely, 'seek common ground while reserving differences'. This was a strategy that could deal with differences at the sub-state level, between states and now in the relations between civilizations. The 2005 White Paper on China's peaceful development outlined the definition and implications of 'diversity of civilizations':

> Diversity of civilizations is a basic feature of human society, an important driving force for the progress of mankind. All countries should respect other country's right to independently choose their own social systems and paths of development, learn from one another and draw on the strong points of others to make up for their own weak points, thus achieving rejuvenation and development in line with their own national conditions. Dialogues and exchanges among civilizations should be encouraged with the aim of doing away with misgivings and estrangement existing between civilizations and develop together by seeking common ground while putting aside differences, so as to make mankind more harmonious and the world more colorful. – jointly build a harmonious world where all civilizations coexist and accommodate one another.[3]

This notion is at once Chinese and internationalist. The notion of 'harmony' squares not only with Zhou Enlai's past principles of diplomacy but also with the UN Charter.

At the 2008 Chinese Olympics opening ceremony, the *'he'* character, used in the compound words for 'peace' and 'harmony', was repeatedly incised on the undulating floor of the 'Bird's Nest' stadium. Hu Jintao's foreign policy has intensely focused on the same notion of 'harmony'. Again the Chinese foreign policy notion of 'harmony without uniformity', or 'harmony without differences' (*he er butong*) correlates with the original

Cold War formulation on 'seeking common ground while reserving differences'.

Chinese statement has been quite explicit on the question of origin. Deng Xiaoping once said that no matter how much international conditions change, Chinese foreign policy will always subscribe to Zhou Enlai's five principles of peaceful coexistence (*heping gongchu wuxiang yuanze*), including equality and mutual benefit, mutual respect for state sovereignty and territorial integrity, non-aggression, non-interference in other states' affairs and peaceful coexistence.[4] These principles together with their companion diplomatic principle, 'seeking common ground while reserving differences' (*qiu tong cunyi*), have provided a continuous basis for China's response to the inevitable 'differences' in international relations.

The Confucian notion of 'harmony with differences' now serves as the cultural origin of Zhou Enlai's 'seeking common ground while reserving differences' and the related formal structure of diplomatic thought provides the contemporary narrative of Chinese foreign policy as China's status changes in world affairs. Rather than 'rising' Chinese foreign policy will focus on the fostering of 'win–win' (*shuangying*) cooperation based upon Chinese values associated with 'harmony'.

The *Renmin ribao* (People's Daily) glossed 'harmony' (*hexie*) expressedly linking Confucian 'harmony' in its traditional connotations of equality and reciprocity with the above foundational principles of Zhou Enlai:

The idea of '*hexie*' or 'harmony' is deeply ingrained in Chinese history; … The character '*he*' in '*hexie*' is written with the character '*he*' meaning 'grain' next to the character '*kou*' meaning mouth, and together they convey the sense that when the people are warm and well-fed, all is harmonious in heaven and earth. The character '*xie*' is written with the character '*yan*' on the left side and '*jie*' on the right side, conveying the meaning that everybody has the right to speak up. Since China's first philosophers advanced the well-known concept of 'harmony is precious', the concept has been handed down from generation to generation. From the Chinese government's *advancement of the five principles of peaceful coexistence* and the idea that all nations big or small are all equal to the advancement of the guiding principle of 'be kind to the neighbours and be partners with the neighbours'...and to its vigorously advocation (sic) of building a new international political and economic order that is fair and reasonable and its advocation of dialogues between different cultures as equals, they all give expression to the idea of harmony.[5]

Such etymological hagiography deserves sustained quotation and analysis as it is actually a matter of high politics. In the initial stages of Hu Jintao's new leadership the principles of 'diplomatic thought' (*waijiao sixiang*) were reviewed. The key question was how best to represent China's standing in the world, especially given the dynamism of China's fast growing economy. This debate saw declining leadership reference to 'China's peaceful rise' (*heping jueqi*) and the elaboration of a 'scientific development concept' to explain entwined domestic and international 'harmonies' based upon the Dengist strategy of 'peace, development and cooperation'.[6] Essentially, Hu Jintao eschewed any radical rethinking of foreign policy. Despite so much change in the world, Hu followed Jiang Zemin in extending the synthesis of the 'diplomatic thought' of Mao Zedong, Zhou Enlai and Deng Xiaoping.[7] Thus Hu continues to dispute the exaggeration of China's new economic power while supporting a more active multilateralism than would have been previously possible. Hu has more latitude to work with, but he still largely operates from within Deng Xiaoping's low foreign policy posture.

Hu Jintao now talks of Chinese-style international relations even as he avoids overweening claims to international leadership. Hu's perspective on deep history as it relates to the character of the Chinese people is somewhat new, but he updates the notion of 'harmony' by synthesizing it with Zhou Enlai's five principles of peaceful coexistence and its operational corollary, 'seeking common ground while reserving differences' together with Deng Xiaoping's 'independent foreign policy' towards 'peace and development'.[8]

Why Hu's particular focus on 'harmony'? 'Harmony' is an easier and more expressively Chinese concept to work with than 'peaceful rise'. It pays a bigger political dividend embracing peace while taking the edge off the potentially threatening connotations of 'rising'. 'Harmony' neatly separates China out from the classical rise and fall of the great powers in the European balance of power and provides a positive basis for contemporary national cohesion. At the same time it expedites a post-Jiang Zemin Party consensus that continues to service Party legitimacy as it connects with economic growth. China participates in 'globalization' while at the same time continuing to support a notion of 'common development' including the North and the South. Moreover, in the lead-up to the Olympics, 'harmony' celebrated the greatness of Chinese civilization, thus supporting a culturally progressive rather than inherently restless and irredentist Chinese nationalism. 'Harmony', in its relation to 'peaceful coexistence', cuts across the past and present to challenge the contemporary notion of the 'China Threat' further to reinforce the positive identification of Chinese nationalism with UN universalism.

Foreign policy is still derivative of the domestic policy focus on development; thus Hu parsed his 'scientific development concept' as it applies to the integration of domestic and international factors in China's passage through the antipodes of globalization:

> ...in the course of China's development both favourable and unfavourable factors will coexist in the international environment for a long time. We must fully exploit the favourable factors, taking the initiative to dispel the unfavourable facts and work hard to change challenges into opportunities. We must adapt to the continual trend of development which is economic globalization.... We must move faster in becoming familiar with international rules and customary practices....[9]

Hu's foreign policy subscribes to an established dialectical approach even if it is 'more activist'.[10] It is not quite the 'new math' suggested by Joshua Cooper Ramo who has talked about the emergence of a 'Beijing Consensus'.[11] Hu does not use the latter term. He has taken a fresh look at the relevance of Chinese history to contemporary policy, but his viewpoint is still largely built on past Party perspective, style and principle. Hu's foreign policy continues to advocate China's 'developing' rather than 'developed' status. In his 15 October 2007 remarks to the 17th National Party Congress, Hu described China as 'a large developing socialist country with an ancient civilization', and he reiterated China's 'goal of building a moderately prosperous society in all respects'.[12]

Chinese foreign policy displays exceptional conceptual continuity and coherence over time. The ideological protestation of continuity is not necessarily a dissembling idealism that obscures an underlying ambition for power. There has been a continuous policy calculation that acts to reduce the costs of external conflict while enhancing the domestic opportunity for development. Since 1949, Chinese foreign policy has treated changing international realities within a self-conscious political framework of 'firm principle and flexibility' that deliberately builds on Party dialectics and political culture. Such thinking values continuity as the basis for political consensus and legitimacy. Party policy and related diplomatic thought prefers to view change from within continuity. The combination of flexibility and principle provided the basis for Deng Xiaoping's ongoing strategy for 'economic reform and the open door' which was rationalized on the ideological basis of Mao's 'seeking the truth from the facts'.[13]

Four generations of Party leaders have self-consciously treated foreign and domestic policy as part of the rolling synthesis of China's foremost priority of national economic development. Most recently, the ancient ideas of 'feeding the people' and 'letting them have their say' were electronically magnified in the symbolism of China's Olympics. The latter's syntax reflected the need for 'inter-civilization coexistence' and the harmony of peoples in their common aspirations for development and happiness.[14]

The five principles continue to serve as the dialectical basis of post-Cold War foreign policy thinking that seeks 'unity' in the recognition of contradictions, but now Zhou Enlai's persona and his wisdom are also deeply rooted in China's ancient 'culture of harmony'. As People's University Professor Zhang Liwen indicated: '[The culture of harmony] is a reflection of the Chinese people's ethical quality and a basic thought of China's modern diplomacy.'[15] In his Harvard address of December 2003, Premier

Wen Jiabao celebrated China's 5,000-year civilization with reference to an abiding cultural intelligence and the importance of contemporary inter-civilization dialogue that progresses on the basis of Zhou Enlai's five principles of peaceful coexistence and 'seeking common ground while reserving differences':

> The Chinese nation has an extremely deep cultural foundation. The Chinese people love peace dearly. 'Harmony with differences' was a great thinking put forward by the Chinese ancient philosophers. [This] kind of harmony is not the run of the mill one. The kind of differences is not the ones that contradict with each other. Harmony is for the sake of living and growing together. Differences are aimed at achieving complementarity. Adopting the '*harmony with differences*' attitude to view and handle problems is not only conducive to our warm treatment of our friendly neighbours, but also to helping defuse *contradictions* in the international community.[16]

While the sustained reference to 'harmony' might be taken as illustrative of Chinese exceptionalism, the reference to harmony is 'for the sake of living and growing together'. The five principles that originated in the Cold War history of decolonization were originally concerned about China's opportunity for development in the context of containment. These principles, rather than supporting the development of alliances, preferred to deal with 'differences' so as to achieve the wider recognition of China and its goal of development. This later provided the basis for a strategy towards globalization.

In his commentary of 19 April 2005, Xiong Guangkai, Director of the China Institute for International Strategic Studies, traced the notion of 'harmony' to the 1955 Bandung Conference: '…the Bandung Conference provided a great historic example of harmonious accommodation of various civilizations and cultures and a convincing denial of the "clash of civilization" theory. It lends immediate significance to the current efforts to promote respect for the world's diversity.'[17]

Premier Wen Jiabao eulogized Zhou Enlai's Bandung thinking of 1955. Although the five principles and the idea of 'reserving differences' originated in the post-Second World War context of new states emerging from colonial dependence, Wen argued that they are now applicable throughout today's international system: 'They are still needed to transcend differences of social system and the unevenness of North–South development and to foster common development.' Wen confirmed that China remains 'an active proponent' and also 'a faithful practitioner of the Five Principles of Peaceful Coexistence' as the latter are 'enshrined in China's Constitution' and serve as 'the cornerstone of China's independent foreign policy'. Wen claimed: 'That the Five Principles of Peaceful Coexistence still have vitality and remain relevant with the passage of time is due, basically speaking to its conformity with the purposes and principles of the UN Charter, with the basic requirements of the development of international relations, and with the fundamental interests of the people in the world.'[18]

Currently, 'harmony with differences', or 'harmony without uniformity' self-consciously parallels Zhou Enlai's 'seeking common ground, while reserving differences'. Underlying Zhou's strategy was a diplomatic directness or style of modesty and honesty. This was the style that had initially appealed to Nehru who joined with Zhou in the original crafting of the five principles. Nehru disagreed with the US policy towards China. He expected that in the long term the rough edges of China's revolution would be smoothed out in the inevitable resurgence of China's ancient civilization.[19]

Even in the 1960s, Western biographers commented on Zhou Enlai's personal grace as if he were the modern reincarnation of the Confucian scholarly gentleman. Zhou's style assumed the direct expression of viewpoint as well as respect for the views of others. The current discussion of 'harmony without uniformity' recalls the ageless wisdom of Confucius. Confucius said: 'A gentleman gets along with others, but does not necessarily agree with them; a base man agrees with others, but does not coexist with them harmoniously.'[20] Hence the rational man does not fear to disagree with others, but does respect different viewpoints. Also, the 'gentleman' in the Chinese tradition makes investigation on the basis of modesty and honesty. The 'mean man' is more likely to agree only to promote an illusion of harmony so as to further his own interest. Such a lesson in moral character may well have informed the drafting of the first Shanghai communiqué when the two sides resorted to an honest statement of 'differences'.

The *Renmin ribao* editorially glossed Hu's 'harmony' highlighting the moral connections between individuals and then moving to the international level of analysis featuring the cooperation between states. The positive nature of 'harmony' is actually embedded in the rational composition of different things' whereas the negativity of 'uniformity' is sterile in 'the simple duplication and coincidence of things of different natures'. Thus the *Renmin ribao* prescribed three principles to facilitate 'harmony without uniformity'. First, the single person ought 'to take his or her own initiative'. Secondly, persons are to allow others to take the initiative; and thirdly, 'one must be good at engaging in friendly cooperation with others'.[21] Substituting states for persons on the basis of 'harmony without uniformity'. This analysis once again emphasized respect for the well established principles of national self-determination and non-interference as well as acceptance of differences as the critical precondition to the creation of a 'harmonious world'.

Over time China's strategy for economic development has undergone basic revision, but all along Chinese foreign policy has been rooted in the priorities of development. This informs the rolling synthesis of ideas linking the various generations of political leaderships in their attempts to focus on national economic development. General Xiong Guangkai, a senior interlocutor of Chinese policy, explained this in 'generational' terms:

...since the founding of New China, the first-generation leadership-collective of the Party with Mao Zedong as the core put forward and jointly initiated together with the leaders of India and Burma as early as in 1954 the five principles of peaceful coexistence. The second-generation...with Comrade Deng Xiaoping as the core put forward the important thesis, 'peace and development are two major issues of the contemporary world' and actively called for the establishment of a new international political and economic order. The third generation...with Jiang Zemin as the core further put forward the establishment of a new security concept of 'mutual trust, mutual benefits, equality and cooperation', [that] called for maintaining the world's diversification and promoting the world's multipolarization and advocated democratization of international relations.[22]

Hu personally threw '*he*' into this dialectical mix of generational wisdom. According to General Xiong, Hu Jintao, in his programmatic speech to the UN in September 2005, accordingly 'held aloft the banner of peace, development and cooperation' and called for ever greater international cooperation on the basis of the five principles of peaceful coexistence.

Hu's September 2005 UN speech dismissed the 'clash of civilizations' in favour of harmony between different civilizations on the basis of 'seeking common ground while reserving differences'. Highlighting 'inclusiveness' in building a 'harmonious world', Hu reasoned:

> Diversity of civilizations is a basic feature of humanity and an important driving force behind human progress. ...various civilizations have made positive contributions to human progress.... Various civilizations can learn from one another and improve together because there are differences. Seeking uniformity with force only leads to the decline and ossification of human civilizations because of a loss of a driving force. There is a difference in the length of history of civilizations, but civilizations cannot be distinguished as superior or inferior.... We should strengthen dialogues and exchanges among different civilizations, learn from each other's strong points to offset one's weaknesses in the course of competition and comparison, *develop together in the course of seeking common ground while reserving differences.*[23]

Such dialectical learning and exchange rejects force in favour of the positive adaptation to civilizational differences. 'Harmony' is thusly synthesized with 'peaceful coexistence'. The internal argument for 'harmony' based on 'coexistence' would have been easy to make within the Party. On the basis of 'coexistence', Chinese policy had witnessed and successfully weathered the collapse of containment, the entry of the PRC into the UN, sequential normalizations with the US, Japan, USSR and Russia, the re-establishment of international trade and open door policies after Tiananmen Square and comparative regional stability in

Central Asia even in the wake of the collapse of the Soviet Union
and the creation of new states in Central Asia.

The Maturation of Chinese Diplomacy

Hu Jintao's 'harmony without uniformity' extends Deng Xiaoping's
'independent foreign policy' based on Zhou Enlai's five principles
and 'seeking common ground while reserving differences'. Deng's
'peace and development' remain at the core of Hu's foreign
policy logic, but is such continuity reasonable and constructive?
Through the years there has been extraordinary change in China's
international environment. Cold War containment collapsed, and
the PRC is playing a prominent role in the UN Security Council.
The Soviet Union has disappeared along with the notion of
'peaceful coexistence' in the US foreign policy. Definitely history
has not ended. China has moved into a brave new world of
'socialist' market reform and is self-consciously participating in
the ever widening process of globalization, even as Hu Jintao
has recently stressed the future importance of China's domestic
market. However, Chinese policy formulation still refers to
different ideologies, systems and approaches to development.

The five principles and the companion corollary to seek common
ground have not only provided the basis for Sino-American
normalization that accepted mutually recognized fundamental
differences, but also provided for the effective management of the
Soviet Union's collapse and subsequent Sino-Russian normalization
as well as for the later formulation of a 'New Security Concept'
(NSC) and the related creation of the new regional forum, the
Shanghai Cooperation Organization.

In May 1991, Jiang Zemin and Mikhail Gorbachev agreed
that Sino-Soviet relations had improved as the result of mutual
application of the five principles.[24] The two sides reiterated the
importance of non-interference and comfortably compared their
respective strategies for reform. Their agreement that the stability
of state and society is necessary to reform was perhaps an *ex
post facto* reflection on Tiananmen Square and the Soviet focus
on the 'normalization of life'. Explicit in their understanding

was not only the substantive principle of non-interference but also the operational imperative to seek common ground, and the two sides also claimed a mutual learning on the basis of a familiar assumption that there are no universal models that fit all national circumstances: 'There are no universal patterns in carrying out reforms. The people of each country have the right to independently decide the affairs of their own country.'[25]

After the highly traumatic collapse of the Soviet Union the five principles were successfully placed at the centre of Sino-Russian relations. The same principles were featured in intergovernmental statements of 29 December 1991 and in late December 1992 when Boris Yeltsin signed the Joint Declaration on the Basic Principles. Yeltsin had travelled to Beijing expecting a sharp rebuke for abandoning communism.[26] He received a warm welcome, and forgetting his earlier reference to the 'communist idol' which had precipitated cruel social discord, Yeltsin recognized that 14 years of Chinese reform could well have relevance for Russia. Despite the vicissitudes of regime change, the five principles bridged the new post-Cold War difference between the two states' political and social systems and provided a coherent framework for dealing with the profound political, security and economic consequences that accompanied the collapse of the Soviet Union. The principles then underwrote China's 'good neighbourly' initiatives in China's post-Soviet Central Asian diplomacy.

The New Security Concept

Since the death of Deng Xiaoping, Chinese diplomacy has engaged in several rounds of diplomatic initiative to facilitate a 'new' understanding of international relations. Chinese diplomacy has endorsed a New Security Concept (*xin anquan guan*) – one that deliberately challenges an old international system ostensibly mired in the inequalities of the balance of power with renewed and upgraded subscription to the core content of the five principles of peaceful coexistence. The latter core has been fast-forwarded to deal with rapid domestic economic change, post-Cold War globalization and the new relevance of non-traditional strategic factors such as terrorism, health crises and the spread of weapons of mass destruction. Chinese diplomacy has called for 'mutual security' (*xianghu anquan*) as opposed to the US notion of 'absolute security' and has taken the five principles out into the world in deliberate political challenge to US 'unilateralism' and pre-emptive force.[27]

The NSC is 'new' in so far as it is a deliberate contrast with the 'old' Western balance-of-power model, but its logic is hardly new to the history of China's diplomatic thought. 'New security' deliberately draws upon the Bandung logic of 'seeking common ground while reserving differences'. National independence and self-determination are still regarded as highly relevant to world politics. Jiang Zemin put this in regional perspective in his speech to the Second APEC Leadership meeting in Malaysia on 11 November 1994: Jiang recommended the application of the five principles of peaceful coexistence in dealing with differences between East Asian nations in their cultural differences and different stages of development.

The five principles approach to differences has been carried forward in the 'Shanghai Spirit' that characterizes the 'new regionalism' of the Shanghai Cooperation Organization (SCO). General Xiong Guangkai, Deputy Chief of the PLA General Staff, elaborated in his 17 August 2004 speech on the SCO and negotiating the differences between states and societies. The following is quoted extensively as it elaborately details the direct connection between contemporary 'Shanghai Spirit' and the five principles of peaceful coexistence:

> One of the substantive connotations of the 'Shanghai Spirit' is the new security concept it advocates – to wit 'mutual trust, mutual benefit, equality and coordination'. Mutual trust means to *put aside the differences in ideology and social system*, to discard the mentality of cold war and power politics.... *Mutual benefit* refers to conforming to the objective demand of social development in the era of globalization, respecting each other's security interests and creating conditions for other parties' security while trying to secure one's own security interests so as to realize security for all. Equality stands for all countries – big or small, strong or weak – being equal

members of the international community, and therefore, should respect each other, treat each other equally and should *not interfere in each other's internal affairs, in order to promote democracy in international relations.* Coordination implies that conflict should be solved through peaceful talks, extensive and deep cooperation should be carried out over security issues of common concern, so as to eliminate hidden worries and head off wars and conflicts. All these four principles are inseparably interconnected to form a complete whole, in which mutual trust stands for the basis, mutual benefit is the aim, equality spells guarantee, while coordination means approach.[28]

The contents of the five principles have not only provided the conceptual basis for the SCO and the NSC, they have been repeatedly cast in explicit alignment with the basic assumptions of the UN Charter, and, as such they '...contain the fundamental values of modern human civilization – peace, equality and human rights'. The universality of these principles is what 'distinguishes them from previous exclusionary philosophies and current unilateralism'.[29]

Development in the Era of Globalization

Moreover, the contemporary foreign policy on 'harmony' correlates with the Chinese approach to development in an era of 'globalization'. Foreign policy highlighting 'harmonious development' insists that China achieve 'development by relying on itself, together with reform and innovation, while persisting in the policy of opening up'.[30] In February 2007, Premier Wen explained the correlation of development that depends 'mainly on [our] efforts and the expansion of China's "opening up to the world"'.

Clearly proclaiming that China's development depends mainly on its own efforts helps to fundamentally eliminate outsiders' suspicions that having reached a certain stage of development, China will go in for external plunder and expansion. If fact, with China developed, it will make ever greater contributions...to the world development.[31]

Wen revives Deng's correlation of the open door with 'self-reliance'. The contemporary reference to 'win–win' may sound like games theory, but at its core is Hu's Confucian notion of 'harmony'. Hu rebuts the claim that the 'China Threat' will become more severe with China's economic development by highlighting an essential 'mutual benefit' as part of the original five principles. Mutual benefit, however, is now interpreted as a correlation of domestic and international harmonies and this correlation projects common development that positively links China's development with that of the world economy.

The above overview of foreign policy formulation, diplomatic thought and events deliberately highlights Chinese foreign policy approach to change from within continuity. If the East–West divide has disappeared substantive differences of ideology, society, religion and culture still persist in world politics. The very persistence of the post-Cold War notion of the 'China Threat' confirms the continued relevance of ideology in international relations. On the other hand, the current relation between peaceful coexistence and harmony affirms a continuity of coherent flexible purpose as suggested in Zhou Enlai's June 1953 observation that any burden for war must be placed on the US.

The Chinese Rebuttal to Realism

What has China been doing in the contemporary context? Some 'realists' argue that China is trying 'to hide its capacities', but that China will inevitably become 'muscular'. John Mearsheimer, for example, dismisses China's formal statements of intent because the underlying reality of unprecedented economic growth will automatically support a natural inclination to rising great power. In other words, there is absolutely no point in the Chinese claiming that they will 'never seek hegemony'. Such talk is 'utterly irrelevant'; 'rising' power, and not peace, is the issue. Mearsheimer contends: 'I think the only way to assess whether China can rise peacefully is with good theory.' Of course, his 'good theory' is Western 'realism'.[32] And this theory offers biological tautology such as: 'As you know when you grow *muscular* you tend to behave differently than when you are weakling.' Mearsheimer's first axiom, 'great powers want to be hegemonic' is exclusive and unidimensional... His second axiom, 'no state can ever be certain about the intentions of other states' is likely premised in the longstanding realist assumption, *si vis pacem, para bellum* (if you want peace, prepare for war). The Chinese notion of 'harmony without uniformity' has dismissed the notion of 'rising', is building on a self-consciously alternative reading of reality, and believes in the political advantage of inclusive diplomacy and the efficacy of 'soft power'.

Former Ambassador and President of China's Foreign Affairs University, Wu Jianmin, replied to Mearsheimer claiming that he had utterly failed 'to understand *the philosophy* of China's modernization'. The Ambassador's rebuttal talked of 'common interests' and 'two preconditions' for China's modernization, namely peace and international cooperation. Wu asked: 'Should China embark on expansionist behaviour what will happen? These two conditions peace and international cooperation would be wiped out.'[33]

The convergence of the five principles with 'harmony without uniformity' projects a non-threatening standpoint that is studiously modest in tone and rational in its positive relation to domestic policy and national self-determination. For Western cynics the Chinese rhetoric on 'harmonious world' may seem no more substantive than beauty pageant expressions of support for world peace. However, the convergence of Chinese principle and flexibility within the synthesis of coexistence and harmony, now provides the basis for a self-consciously modest and arguably effective, if perhaps understated leadership role within regional and international organization.[34] Hu's diplomacy aligns particularly well with the priorities of national economic development as these correlate with respect for national self-determination. Such diplomacy supports China's development by exercising a cost efficient option that eschews alliances and arms race, not to mention the uncertain complications and costs of pre-emptive force in dealing with the unresolved asymmetries of power in world politics.

For the last several years China has been engaged in an active diplomatic offensive that looks forward to a 'harmonious world' based on the historical lessons of 'peaceful coexistence'. China's principles champion an alternative international approach that challenges US foreign policy assumptions. To see this only as a 'charm offensive' that represents a superficial paean to world peace is to ignore how the substance of this foreign policy supports the extension of China's soft power.

In his programmatic 2005 speech on lasting peace and common prosperity at the UN's 60th anniversary, President Hu Jintao referred to the UN's 'beautiful ideal' of economic and social development, the favourable trend towards the New Security Concept, and the importance of the 'spirit of inclusiveness' in the progressive adaptation to the 'diversity of civilizations'. Hu also referred to the developmental importance of 'the mutual learning of respective strong points instead of making a fetish out of a particular model'. He identified the UN with China's thematic emphases on peace and development, 'democratized international relations' and 'harmonious coexistence' in such a way as to extend the five principles of peaceful coexistence and 'seeking common ground while reserving differences' through the 'scientific' application of Party work-style based on modesty and criticism and self-criticism.[35]

Subsequently, the December 2005 White Paper on the Peaceful Development Road 'looked back on history' and summed up China's foreign policy of peaceful development on the basis of four generalizations as to China's future direction. Firstly, China has to strive 'for a peaceful international environment to develop itself and promoting world peace through its own development'. Secondly, the White Paper built upon Deng's original formulation of 'self-reliance and the open door'. Self-reliance requires 'development by [China] relying on itself together with reform and innovation, while persisting in the policy of opening up'. This injunction accords with the ongoing attempt to protect 'socialism with Chinese characteristics' as against Western 'peaceful evolution' and highlights the aforementioned renewed policy focus on China's domestic market as insurance against the vicissitudes of globalization and the global marketplace. Thirdly, policy reiterated the importance of 'conforming to the trend of economic globalization and striving to achieve mutually beneficial common development with other countries'. Fourthly, China was to work with other countries in building a 'harmonious world' through 'peace, development and cooperation'.[36]

Chinese policy builds on Deng's 'open door', 'inviting in' (qingjinlai) foreign firms at an accelerated rate and more recently promoting 'walking out' (zhouchuqu) Chinese firms into international markets.[37] To use the well known language of Nye and Keohane's theory of 'interdependence', Chinese foreign policy tolerates a degree of sensitivity as it dialectically sifts the liabilities and opportunities of 'globalization', but vulnerability is still unacceptable.

Hu Jintao participates in the rolling synthesis of Chinese diplomatic thought. He has more or less followed Deng's instruction to keep a low profile in the world while making a positive contribution to world affairs. In February 2007 Premier Wen Jiabao reiterated the Chinese strategy of change from within continuity as it works to enhance China's developmental opportunities, and he added: 'Precisely by not raising our banner or taking the lead initially we've been able to expand our room for manoeuvre in international affairs.'[38]

In his 15 October 2007 speech to the 17th National Party Congress, Hu Jintao again reprised his multidimensional approach to harmony:

> We maintain that the people of all countries should join hands and strive to build a harmonious world of lasting peace and common prosperity. To this end, all countries should uphold the purposes and principles of the UN charter, observe international law and universally recognized norms of international relations, and promote democracy, harmony, collaboration and win-win solutions in international relations. Politically, all countries should respect each other...and endeavour to promote democracy in international relations. Economically, they should cooperate with each other, draw on each other's strengths and work together to advance economic globalization in the direction of balanced development shared

benefits and win–win progress. Culturally, they should learn from each other in the *spirit of seeking common ground while shelving differences*, respect the diversity of the world and make joint efforts to advance human civilization.[39]

Chinese foreign policy thinking is an ongoing dialectic that self-consciously combines principle and flexibility. This is not only an important matter of domestic politics, but is conceivably a welcome basis for the emergence of new power on the world stage. Arguably, Chinese 'pragmatism' is constructive in its domestic focus on development and national self-determination.

'Revisit the Past and Know New Things'

Moreover, while the contemporary leadership's reading of Chinese history is not especially professional; it is not so exclusively tied to the history of the Chinese revolution, and to China's historical role as victim. China's imperial and modern history has been placed at the service of regional and international stability. Chinese nationalism has become increasingly comfortable with universalism as world 'harmony'.

The interpretation of Chinese nationalism from within the 'diversity of civilizations' militates against an inherently aggressive sense of unique national destiny. Historically, this was not always the case. Sun Yatsen, for example, was intense in his focus on Chinese nationalism, as the most 'precious possession by which humanity maintains its existence'. His nationalism rejected both the 'cosmopolitanism' of China's universal empire and the distractions of American and British 'cosmopolitanism' that negate China's nation-building and mask the hidden agenda of foreign material civilization.[40] In contrast, Hu Jintao's 'harmony' brings Chinese nationalism together with internationalism.

In an analysis of China's 'model' for international relations this chapter emphasizes the origins and contemporary strategic implications of 'harmony' as the basis for Hu Jintao's formal foreign policy thinking. Hu's correlation of domestic and international harmonious development reinforces the established subordination of foreign to domestic policy. Hu has taken advantage of the victory of the five principles over containment and realist balance-of-power thinking. Hu's notion of 'harmony' continues the Chinese challenge to balance of power politics, and it specifically challenges the 'clash of civilizations' in its advocacy of the 'diversity of civilizations' and 'harmony without uniformity'. The correlation of Chinese nationalism and civilization with UN universalism challenges the realist understanding of 'rising' power. 'Harmony' serves as a politically formidable rebuttal to the 'China Threat' in any hard sense of applied military force, but it is certainly congenial to the spread of Chinese 'soft power'.

The above interpretation of events and foreign policy concerning containment, normalization and expanding participation in regional and international multilateralism largely agrees with Wen Jiabao's assertion that the Cold War principles and strategy that trumped original containment are still relevant in today's post-Cold War conditions of economic globalization. China's deliberate dialectics of learning still provide the framework for policy based upon flexible adaptation to extraordinary international change. Western 'realism', on the other hand, is impatient with formally stated Chinese foreign policy thinking. It interprets Chinese reference as part of a disassembling strategy to distract the unwitting observer from the underlying Chinese motivations for power. This perspective underestimates the political importance of diplomacy and neglects analysis of domestic politics and history as part of the explanation for Chinese foreign policy thinking.

There is a new trend in China to learn from Chinese history, hence the idea of *wen gu er zhi xin*, or 'revisit the past and know new things'.[41] While Mao had instructed 'make the past serve the present' (*yi gu wei jin*), the past in Mao's day was a source of revolutionary ambivalence. Now the deep past is playing a more positive role in the Chinese view of the world. Chinese history is no longer the total sum of peasant revolt and colonial victimization. The celebration of Chinese civilization complements the national and the international focus on 'peace and development'. In an era when reform has transcended class struggle, Confucianism has been conscripted in the positive identification of Chinese nationalism with Chinese civilization. The latter is ancient, but in its current manifestation it is not self-consciously imperial. In today's world civilizations are expected to learn from one another. Chinese civilization is not a unique manifestation of superior culture; it has become part of the 'diversity of civilizations'.

'Harmony without uniformity' looks forward to world politics that encourages the diplomatic recognition of respectful disagreement and also mutual cooperation in common development based on the original wisdom of 'seeking common ground while reserving differences'. 'Without uniformity' invokes the post-Bandung success of 'seeking common ground while reserving differences'. The differences of 'civilization' are now 'reserved' under the contemporary 'democratization of international relations'. The reservation of differences deliberately supports 'common development', whereas the advocacy of a single model of development is viewed as a rigid negativity that conflicts with 'national independence and self-reliance'.

Deng Xiaoping's legacy, as it eschews extravagant claims of world leadership and challenges the dysfunctional military and political costs of leadership at the expense of national economic development, still stands. In Ambassador Wu Jianmin's words, American 'realist' analysis, as it promotes the 'China Threat', has utterly failed to understand the philosophy underlying China's national economic development. Development and not 'rising' is the issue. Indeed, a Chinese foreign policy that acknowledges and accommodates 'differences' while focusing on 'common ground' and 'common development' is just as politically important in today's globalizing world as it was in Bandung in 1955.

6

CHINA REDUX?

Chinese adaptation to the world has been a matter of deliberate dialectical learning that critically explores the synthesis of experience and values on the inside and outside of China. Enormous change has been digested and analysed from within this framework of continuous learning. Moreover, a lot of what the Chinese have learned has come from the outside. While the Chinese do like to emphasize 'Chinese characteristics', one has to note that the key vocabulary that connects modern China with the world, such as 'socialism', 'Marxism-Leninism', rule of law, human rights and democracy, are all essentially Western in origin. Also, these terms have become integral to the reform discourse inside China despite the often obvious lack of any significant equivalence in the Chinese tradition.

The Learning Dialectic and the Strategy for Development

In placing China in the world, the Party's learning dialectic has expedited a rather successful open-ended approach to national economic development as it is contextualized in changing domestic and international conditions. Mao Zedong moved well beyond the limitations of the late-nineteenth-century strategy of 'Chinese learning as substance, Western learning for use' (*zhongxue wei ti, xixue wei yong*). This limited *ti-yong* strategy allowed only the import of science and technology for the expressed purposed of protecting the unique moral dimensions of Chinese civilization. This strategy was purely defensive. It was designed to avoid the contamination of the core of Chinese civilization from a competitive state system that was predicated in power and profit. There was no real 'open door' in this.

In August 1956, Mao specifically disagreed with the *ti-yong* strategy. In learning from other countries he eschewed 'dogmatism' and 'conservatism'. Neither mechanical copying of outside culture, ideas and experience nor insistence on Chinese 'exceptionalism' was appropriate to his dialectical thinking. Perhaps even more surprising, given prevailing Cold War assumptions concerning the unbreakable bond of socialist fraternity between Moscow and Beijing, Mao pointed out that his Soviet comrades had made 'grave mistakes of principle'. Mao gave them a failing grade for their dialectics. At the same time he heartily disliked US imperialism. Mao was, nevertheless, prepared to learn about the 'strong points' of both the Soviet Union and the US.

Mao urged the study of foreign things to improve Chinese things, but he also expressed strong reservation against 'mechanical copying'; thus he said, 'Studying things foreign isn't equivalent to copying them all.' Mao also went beyond the *ti-yong* understanding when he accepted the possibilities of synthesis. He stated: 'We must study each side well, the Chinese and the foreign. Doing the two things by half will not do. We've got to take the two half measures and turn them into two wholes.' Mao emphasized: 'This isn't the same as taking "Chinese learning as the substance, Western learning for practical use." By "learning" we mean the basic principles, which are applicable everywhere and shouldn't be differentiated as "Chinese" or "foreign".'[1]

After 1949 and particularly in 1956 and again in 1978, the CCP took the view that '*ti*' (essence) can be selectively applied in China as a matter of open-ended but deliberately critical synthesis of Chinese and outside concepts and ideas about society, political culture, institutions, economic strategy, etc. Adaptation to the outside world was not predicated in a deliberate sense of superiority, but on Chinese cultural predisposition to modest, but certainly not self-effacing study.

This is why, for example, in the recent White Paper on building democracy it indicates that there is no universal model that is to prevail in all times and places. Almost as if to repeat Pearl

Buck's characterization, the White Paper stated that 'The Chinese people are industrious, courageous and full of wisdom.' For this reason the 'mechanical copying' of American liberal democracy is especially unlikely, but some degree of synthesis is still possible, hence the White Paper included reference to adaptation to 'Western democracy':

> In building socialist political democracy, China has always adhered to the basic principle that the Marxist theory of democracy be *combined with the reality of China, borrowed from the useful achievements of the political civilization of mankind, including Western democracy,* and assimilated the democratic elements of China's traditional culture and institutional civilization. Therefore, China's socialist political democracy shows distinctive Chinese characteristics.[2]

While Chinese nationalism has strenuously objected to 'blind Westernization', reform in China has been able to use qualitatively important foreign concepts on the basis of the dialectical sifting of the positives and negatives of foreign experience as it might relate to Chinese conditions. Such understanding should inform the interpretation of 'Chinese characteristics'. The latter came about from within a deliberate learning dialectic that eschewed extreme nationalism in favour of a modest, but self-confidently critical adaptation to the outside world. Just as, for example, in Chapter 3, when the jurists speak of the need for integrating 'interior' and 'exterior correlations' and synthesizing 'internationalization and localization'. 'Chinese characteristics' are not borne of a brooding aggressive nationalism, but are a routine part of the ongoing synthesis of domestic and foreign ideas that impact states and societies in the contemporary age of globalization.

Even in the highly contentious area of 'human rights', Deng Xiaoping originally suppressed domestic attempts to identify with this terminology as it was identified as a contemptuous part of Western strategies of 'peaceful evolution' or 'disintegration' that were designed to undermine the legitimacy of 'Chinese socialism with Chinese characteristics'. In this instance, Deng apparently allowed ideology to stand in the way of critical learning. Deng, however, got over his personal indignation and there was a subsequent paradigm shift in policy. 'Human rights' subsumed citizens' rights and were recognized as applicable to China. Chinese diplomacy then insisted that China has the right to participate in international discourse as to the development of the contents of international categories of human rights.

The identification and analysis of this Chinese learning dialectic is important to the interpretation of how Chinese policy sees China in the world. The origins of learning from the strong points of all countries were contemporaneous with the development of the strategy of the five principles of peaceful coexistence that were originally designed to break down the barriers of containment. Peace was deliberately sought so as to focus on the number one priority, national economic development. Measured Chinese response was not imperial. Its logic was highly rational in its deliberately modest and selective adaptation to China's own realities.

Containment had to be overcome in order to secure national economic development; and the potential for learning was so much greater as the walls of containment came tumbling down. Deng went to the UN, and, in his landmark 1974 speech to the General Assembly, he insisted on the distinction between self-reliance and autarchy.[3] 'Self-reliance' (*zili gengsheng*), which carries connotations of 'self-standing' and 'turning over the body', argued that the fundamentals of the economy are to be China-based, but Deng hastened to add that this still allowed for increased participation in international trade and investment in support of national economic development.

Deng did not throw China's door wide open. As he experimented, he carefully opened the door a bit at a time. Deng wanted critical adaptation to the outside world, hence he brought together the notion of 'self-reliance' and the 'open door'. This strategy was predicated in Zhou and Mao's original perspective that while China could benefit from international exchange, China's national economic development could not depend on the resources and experience of other countries.

This openness based on critical study was reflected in later positive but cautious adaptation to globalization which Chinese leaders often described as a 'double-edged sword' (*shuang jiandao*). Chinese analysis has not harboured extreme nationalism. It has not lost sight of globalization's impact on sovereignty, but it treats globalization as part of the international trend towards peace and development.[4] Such underlying calculation has supported China's rational engagement with the world economy and as a result of related policies China is arguably in a much better position to make a contribution to the contemporary process of international economic recovery.

'Reform as Revolution'?

What about the choice between socialism and capitalism? Deng claimed that 'reform is revolution'. In this light, contemporary special economic zones become yesterday's border regions. Deng described them as if there were new place for applying the original border region concept, 'seeking the truth from the facts'. He said: 'A special economic zone is a medium for introducing technology, management and knowledge.'[5] The learning dialectic in either case had to foster bold experiment in dealing with socio-economic realities. Reform experiment was for the purposes of achieving 'socialism with Chinese characteristics'.

During the Cultural Revolution, Deng had been bitterly denounced for espousing the 'theory of productive forces'. During the first several years of reform, as Deng groped for stones on the river bed, the related contradictions of 'socialism' versus 'capitalism' seemed to become increasingly 'antagonistic'. Deng, himself, had originally focused everyone's attention on the more serious nature of 'leftist' rather than 'rightist' mistakes when 'bourgeois liberalization' reached the boiling point in 1989. Deng put down the counterrevolutionary 'turmoil', outflanked the leftists, defended the correctness of economic reform and the open door and then proceeded with an accelerated reform that called for extraordinary structural changes to facilitate the wholesale adaptation to the 'socialist market'.

Deng 'liberated' the productive forces and touted the 'socialist market' as the 'fundamental mechanism' for distribution. Also in the 1980s and 1990s, there was a major revision to the principle of 'each according to his/her own work' and, as discussed in Chapter 5, this has been followed in the last decade by changes to ownership and a controversy over 'equality of protection' as it concerns public and private ownership and the potential extension of the 'right of use' in the countryside and the superiority of public ownership under 'socialism'.

As the contradictions of reform continually accumulated, it pushed further and further an experimentalism that was justified in 'seeking the truth from the facts', as the epitome of the wisdom of the four generations of leadership, but it is likely that Mao's generation would never have accepted today's 'pluralized' distribution and ownership and that they would have raised objection to a historical focus on 'harmony'. Under such thinking it almost seems as if social justice is the outcome of an eternal characteristic of Chinese culture rather than the outcome of the contradiction between productive forces and productive relations. The 'socialist market', for example, has become a 'neutral' technical mechanism rather that a reflection of social conflict.

'Democratization of International Relations' and 'Diversity of Civilizations'

In the above terms of reference, where is the threat to the world order? The long-term process of overcoming containment and China's subsequent anti-China threat diplomacy has fostered 'national independence and self-reliance' on the basis of a critical but open-ended concept of dialectical learning that in its essence is neither assertive nor aggressive. Historically, such learning built upon the five principles of peaceful coexistence, and *qiu tong cunyi*, which, themselves, connect with the European origins of the Westphalian system in so far as it positively features reciprocity and equality between sovereign states. It is on this basis that contemporary Chinese foreign policy claims that there is a positive correlation between China's foreign policy principles and those enshrined in the UN Charter.

The continual development of this learning dialectic as it relates to the extension of the five principles to include today the 'democratization of international relations' and the 'diversity of civilizations' currently recommends a 'new' model of international relations. The Chinese approach to 'models' as discussed in the last chapter is deliberately open-ended and allows for the possibilities of synthesis while recognizing local differences and sensibilities and carefully avoiding any conceptual imperialism that might challenge any particular national model. The Chinese position at bottom is that there can be any number of legitimate models, and this 'model' of international relations is especially relevant to today's increasingly complex world where there is a growing reaction against preemptive unilateralism and costly misguided military force.

This elastic 'model' builds upon a critique of an 'old' model that was utterly lacking in reciprocity and was self-avowedly predicated in hierarchal notions of power and threat. At least in their experience, CCP leaders believed that the balance of power system of great power politics was inherently dysfunctional in its undermining of national self-determination and sovereign state equality. Their foreign policy is actually very interesting in its self-conscious rejection of 'realism' and in its alternative advocacy of common security. Chinese security analysis has challenged Western 'realism' for its exclusive focus on capability as an end in and of itself. Capability then is open to highly selective and self-interested interpretation and it can only be correlated with threat.

A senior researcher at the influential Institute of International and Strategic Studies has argued that any genuine calculation of threat ought to be ascertained on the basis of a complex understanding of national and international realities. Such calculation ought to take into account military strategic guidelines, actual strategic objectives and the underpinnings of foreign policy. Official statement of purpose has to be thrown into this mix together with other variables and not simply dismissed as the unstated art of deception.[6]

Also, Central Party School analysis has suggested that there must be a 'sense of propriety in the handling of international relations'. This 'propriety' extols balance and compromise, but not concession. It avoids absolute winning in favour of flexible learning about 'the *dialectical relationship* between competition and compromise'.[7] Such perspective accords with leadership perspective on avoiding 'absolute security' and the alternative need for building common security on the inclusive basis of reciprocity and equality of sovereign states that all have security needs.

Four generations of CCP leaders have all believed in China's independence and self-reliance and have refused to accept 'blind Westernization' and are especially suspicious of 'liberal democracy'. On the other hand, Deng Xiaoping, Jiang Zemin and Hu Jintao have all insisted on China's participation in international human rights discourse, and they have encouraged a deep reform process that is exploring the domestic legislative application of international human rights law and related tentative institutional development that concerns the cognate correlations of the rule of law, human rights and democracy. These key terms of reference are Western in origin, but this has all been done with reference to 'Chinese characteristics'.

The Learning Dialectic and Hu's 'Scientific Development Concept'

Hu Jintao's leadership now refers to the Party's well established learning process as a 'scientific development concept' (*kexue fazhan guan*) that is inspired by the desire to create a 'harmonious society' (*hexie shehui*). In the past Mao's China was all about contradiction. 'Harmony' is now celebrated as a quintessential Chinese notion that speaks to the cultural characteristics of the Chinese people. China will participate in international development and globalization, but it will do so on the basis of self-reliance and national independence. In Hu Jintao's view this is how domestic and international harmony will come together.

This view reflects a maturation of perspective that supports Chinese participation in world affairs. China's victimization by imperialism is still remembered as China continues to support the Third World, but history is becoming more than the modern episode of treaty ports and civil war, it is also about an ancient civilization that now informs modern China and interacts with other civilizations on the basis of reciprocity and equality. China still insists on the five principles of peaceful coexistence as they support harmony and on the modesty that is implied in the learning dialectic that has been sponsored by the 'four generations' of leadership.

Sorting out the continuities and discontinuities that have been generated in the application of their learning dialectic is not easy. The Chinese leadership, itself, has not applied 'seeking the truth from the facts' to construct a distinctive inventory of 'Chinese characteristics'. The latter are raised in specific practical context. Moreover, the contemporary canvas of Chinese understanding is a bit like an Indian palimpsest. One sees the welter of past calligraphy lying just beneath the new Chinese characters of modern China.

The learning dialectic, itself, immediately originates with Marxist-Leninist analysis during the revolutionary years. It was 'sinified' through the general relation of Marxist-Leninist theory to praxis within the context of China's national conditions. At times Mao's dialectical learning seemed to connect directly with the traditional Chinese *yin-yang* dialectics.[8] Chapter 2 discussed how Mao in 1956–58 forgot his own notion of 'seeking the truth from the facts'. In the disastrous context of the Great Leap Forward, the Soviets dismissed Mao as a Chinese peasant who was addicted to 'hurrah communism' and whose failed analysis was rooted in a crude traditional Chinese dialectics. Professor Klaus Mehnert summed up the views of Soviet writers on Mao's 'wild chauvinism' as it connects with his native Daoism:

Mao's skilful utilization of the Chinese passion for quotations is said to have nothing in common with dialectics, but to derive instead from primitive Chinese folk philosophy. Mao's aversion to book learning is said to have been inherited from the ancient sages. For instance, Lao Tse: 'It is difficult to rule a nation which possesses much knowledge.' Mao said: The more books one reads, the dumber one gets.[9]

When Deng finally met Gorbachev in Beijing on 16 May 1989 he acknowledged that 'there was a lot of empty talk on both sides'.[10] Now that the past is less of an ideological liability, Chinese commentary is less encumbered in its discussion of Mao's roots in the Chinese traditional culture and this commentary easily debates the adaptation of Marxist-Leninist dialectics to the *yin-yang* philosophical tradition. Also, Deng Xiaoping's 'seeking the truth from the facts' provides an interesting stylistic parallel with the early-nineteenth-century school of imperial 'statescraft', particularly as the latter reacted to the formalism of officials and alternatively stressed the practical solution of political problems on the basis of the slogan, 'learning of practical use to society'.[11]

Contemporary foreign policy also makes much more comment on its connection with China's ancient civilization. Perspectives on conflict and cooperation and the importance of avoiding war if at all possible have been conscripted in the explanation of China's contemporary international relations. The contemporary Hu Jintao historiography has, for example, suggested that Zhou Enlai's style and principles of diplomacy reflected that of the classical *junzi*, or Chinese gentleman.

There is, however, a sharp departure from tradition in the CCP's history of the modern Chinese revolution. In particular, modern perspective focuses on the equality of nation states in their enjoyment of national self-determination. There is no room in this for a 'Middle Kingdom', and the emphasis on equality is the key to the development of contemporary notions of the 'diversity of civilizations', the 'pluralization of models of development', and the 'democratization of international relations' as well as in the New Security Concept which recommends a notion of community security that builds on 'equal security' as opposed to the 'absolute security' that is ascribed to the US.

The Party's 'Chinese Characteristics'?

Deng Xiaoping once said: 'If any problem arises in China, it will arise from inside the Communist Party.'[12] Possibly the most important inscription of a Chinese characteristic in our palimpsest of the past and present is the Party, itself. The Party organized a revolution against the hierarchical nature of Confucian society. In theory, the Party preferred the collective wisdom of the masses to the absolute morality of the 'Son of Heaven', but, in practice, the CCP has often acted like a mentoring custodial elite that knows better than masses especially when it comes to the hard to understand twists and turns of China's politics.

The Party's mass line has recently been updated by Hu Jintao who speaks of its inherently 'scientific' approach to leadership, workstyle and participation. Hu's leadership extols a familiar workstyle that insists on a careful dialectical reading of developing contradictions. Such workstyle extols essentially traditional values of honesty and modesty in its acceptance of mistakes on the basis of the universal fallibility of man. However, while the Party has at times incisively critiqued the past, the Party has still had to struggle for most of the twentieth century with the 'spirit of the leader'.

Deng Xiaoping, in 1956, took on the highly sensitive responsibility for the revision of the Party Constitution and documents to ensure against the occurrence in China of a Stalin-like personality cult. Again, in 1978, Deng stepped in to debunk Hua Guofeng's 'two whatevers' and insist on a new strategy of institutionalization that would entwine 'democratization and legalization' so as to control for the unpredictable and anti-democratic notion of personality cult. The Party was mobilizing its own members and the general public on the need to understand the rule of law, when Deng returned out of semi-retirement to lead a group of presumably wise and experienced veterans to denounce and replace a duly established Party leadership in 1989. Paradoxically, in the immediate past of reform politics, while Deng's own strategy of institutionalization recommended 'acting according to law', it may have taken some element of spirited leadership to galvanize Party reformers to accelerate economic reform and to defend the learning dialectic that has witnessed China's integration with the outside world.

There is no one left of the veteran revolutionary generation who could possibly fill the shoes of Mao, or Deng. The CCP is going to have to achieve new organizational resilience without the benefit of the 'spirit of the leader'. There are no more 'great helmsmen'. Contemporary politics has more opportunity to focus intently on the 'ruling Party' in the context of the development of a 'spiritually' unimpeded strategy of institutionalization. And this should also affect how the Party connects the rule of law, human rights and democracy.

Indeed, the inscription of the character for 'harmony' on the Olympic floor of the Bird's Nest was meant to be symbolic in its connection of the deep past with the Chinese present in today's context of globalization. China's rise or *resurgam* has often been a careful matter of internal reflection and strategic learning. Moreover, the internal focus on the creation of a Chinese form of governance appears to have reached a new stage of organizational development with the current leadership's expanded 'scientific' institutional strategy, to promote 'harmony' in dealing with the underlying stresses and strains of the deepening reform in society and the economy. In this prospect, there is likely to be a more pronounced and developed correlation of political and economic reform that deliberately synthesizes Western and Chinese characteristics so as to facilitate national economic development.

NOTES

Preface

1. John K. Fairbank, *United States and China*. Cambridge, Mass.: Harvard University Press, 1951.
2. For discussion on related international debate in education see Ronald C. Keith, 'The Canadian Study of "Asia"', *Canadian Journal of Development Studies*, vol. iii, no. 2, October 1982, p. 372.
3. John Lindbeck, *Understanding China*. New York, Washington and London: Praeger Publishers, 1971, p. 17.
4. Ibid., p. 47.
5. Ronald C. Keith, 'Transcript of Discussions with Wu Daying and Zhang Zhonglin Concerning Legal Change and Civil Rights', *The China Quarterly*, no. 81, March 1980, pp. 111–21. Wu Daying in the wake of the later Tiananmen Square event in 1989 became director of the key Institute of Political Science.
6. John Bryan Starr, *Understanding China*, revised and updated edition. New York: Hill & Wang, 2001.
7. Francis Fukuyama, 'How the Academy Failed the Nation: The Decline of Regional Studies', *SAIS Bulletin*, 2004.
8. This new view on history was considered in my keynote speech to the Third International Symposium on Zhou Enlai Studies, Nankai University, April 2008. See R. Keith, 'The Contemporary Relevance of Zhou Enlai's Diplomacy of Peaceful Coexistence' (*Dui Zhou Enlai heping gongchu waijiaode dangdai pingjia*), 20 April 2008. In R. Keith's *The Diplomacy of Zhou Enlai* (London and New York: St Martin's Press, 1989), there was some preliminary discussion of Zhou and the Confucian doctrine of the 'golden mean' (pp. 2–3), but there was no explicit interpretation correlating the Confucian notion of 'harmony' with the five principles and their corollary, 'seek common ground while reserving differences'.
9. See, for example, *White Papers of the Chinese Government* (Zhongguo zhengfu bai pishu), vols i–iv. Beijing: Foreign Languages Press, 2000–05.
10. John K. Fairbank, *The United States and China*. Cambridge, Mass. and London: Harvard University Press, 1983, p. xvii.

1 Understanding China Once More

1. John K. Fairbank, Edwin Reischauer and Albert Craig, *East Asia Traditional and Transformation*. Boson: Houghton Mifflin, 1978, p. 486.
2. Conrad Schirokauer and Donald Clark, *Modern East Asia*, second edition. Boston and New York: Houghton Mifflin Company, 2008, pp. 154–5.
3. See under 'Fukuzawa Yukichi', in Charles Lanman, *Japan: Its Leading Men*. Boston: D. Lothrop Co., 1886, pp. 46–7.
4. Gilbert Rozman distinguished between several types of Confucianism including 'imperial Confucianism' and 'elite Confucianism'. The latter concerned the samurai's opportunistic appropriation of Confucian teachings so as to strengthen their elite position in society. His analysis also makes useful reference to a Chinese 'reform Confucianism' that originated with a late imperial notion of 'statescraft' (*qing shi*). This book's concluding chapter suggests that this statescraft provided some historical basis for modern Deng Xiaoping 'pragmatism'. Gilbert Rozman, 'Comparisons of Modern Confucian Values in China and Japan', in Gilbert Rozman, ed., *The East Asian Region: Confucian Heritage and its Modern Adaptation*. Princeton, N.J.: Princeton University Press, pp. 164–5.
5. Chang Chih-tung (Zhang Zhidong), *China's Only Hope*. Trans. Samuel Woodbridge. Westport, Conn.: Hyperion Press, 1975, pp. 32–3. The missionary translation here would seem to pose a number of problems. 'Religion', for example, may mean Confucianism as a philosophy and way of life. 'Race' was commonly used to imply 'nation'.
6. Tsou Jung (Zou Rong), *The Revolutionary Army: A Chinese Revolutionary Tract of 1903*, introduction and translation by John Lust. The Hague and Paris: Mouton & Co., 1968, p. 68.
7. Ibid., pp. 80–1.
8. Frank Goodnow, *China: An Analysis*. New York: Arno Press, 1979, reprint of 1926 original published by the Johns Hopkins University Press, pp. 275–6.
9. Ibid., p. 278, author's italics. For analysis of contemporary opinion that saw China as a threat even in the context of the 'zenith' of European and American imperialism see Jerome Ch'en, *China and the West: Society and Culture 1815–1937*. London: Hutchinson & Co., 1979, p. 50.
10. Lecture Three on Nationalism, Sun Yatsen, *Sanminzhuyi* (The Three People's Principles), trans. by Frank Price, edited by L.T. Chen. Shanghai: Institute of Pacific Relations, 1927, Taipei, 1953 reprint, p. 17.

11. See the fifth lecture under Part II: The Principle of Democracy in Sun Yatsen, *Sanminzhuyi*, pp. 112–13.
12. May-Ling Soong Chiang (Jiang Meiling Song), *China Shall Rise Again*. New York and London: Harper & Brothers Publishers, c1941, p. 7.
13. Mao certainly approved of this view. See Samuel Griffith's translation and introduction relating to this, *Sun Tzu: The Art of War*. London: Oxford University Press, 1973, p. 50.
14. See Confucius' discussion in 'The Great Learning' (*Daxue*), in *Sishu* (Four Books). Trans. by Chen Wei. Juwen tang chubanshe, 1962.
15. *Discourses on Salt and Iron*, trans. by Esson M. Gale. Taipei: Ch'eng Wen Publishing Company, 1973, pp. 5.
16. Soong, *China Shall Rise Again*, p. 23.
17. Cited in Michael Hunt, 'Chinese National Identity and the Strong State; The Late Qing – Republican China', in Lowell Dittmer and Samuel Kim, eds, *China's Quest for National Identity*. Ithaca: Cornell University Press, 1991, p. 71.
18. Mao Tse-tung, 'On New Democracy', in *Selected Works of Mao Tse-tung*, vol. ii. Beijing: Foreign Languages Press, 1965.
19. Mao Tse-tung, 'Speech at the Enlarged Session of the Military Affairs Committee and the External Affairs Committee' (11 September 1959), in Stuart R. Schram, ed., *Mao Tse-tung Unrehearsed*. Harmondsworth: Penguin Books Ltd, 1975, pp. 153–4.
20. Pearl S. Buck, *China As I See It*, compiled and edited by Theodore Harris. London: Methuen and Co. Ltd, 1971, p. 9.
21. Charles Krauthammer, 'Why America Must Contain China', *Time*, 31 July 1995, p. 52.
22. Steven Mosher, *China's Plan to Dominate Asia and the World*. San Francisco: Encounter Books, 2000, p. 1.
23. Ibid., p. 75.
24. For the foreign policy implications of this see Ronald C. Keith, 'The Origins and Strategic Implications of China's "Independent Foreign Policy"', *International Journal*, vol. xli, no. 1, Winter 1985–86, pp. 95–128.
25. John Lindbeck, *Understanding China*. New York, Washington and London: Praeger Publishers, 1971, p. 17.

2 Fitting the People's Republic of China Into the World

1. Zhou Enlai, *Selected Works of Zhou Enlai*, vol. iii. Beijing: Foreign Languages Press, p. 100. Compare with Zhou Enlai, *Zhou Enlai Xianji*. Beijing: Renmen chubanshe, 1984.
2. Ibid., p. 96.

3. 'Chou En-lai Writes Article in Honor of 10th Anniversary of New China', NCNA English, Peking, *Current Background*, 6 October 1959, p. 6.
4. Special Representative of the Central People's Government of the People's Republic of China at the United Nations, *China Accuses*. Peking: Foreign Languages Press, 1951, p. 3.
5. Ibid., p. 93.
6. Ibid., p. 97.
7. Zhou Enlai, *Selected Works of Zhou Enlai*, vol. ii, p. 99.
8. As cited in Shu Guangzhang, 'Constructing 'Peaceful Coexistence: China's Diplomacy toward the Geneva and Bandung Conferences, 1954–55', *Cold War History*, vol. 7, no. 4, (November 2007), p. 513.
9. Zhou Enlai, *Selected Works of Zhou Enlai*, vol. iii, p. 78.
10. Ibid., p. 79.
11. Ibid., p. 159.
12. Ibid., p. 165.
13. Ronald C. Keith, *The Diplomacy of Zhou Enlai*. London: Macmillan, 1989, p. 98. This book is in Chinese translation, see Keith, *Zhou Enlaide waijiao shengya* (Zhou Enlai's Diplomatic Career). Beijing: Central Committee Party School Press, 1990.
14. *Zhonghua ren min gongheguo dui wai guanxi wenjiajianji*, 54–5, (Collected documents on the foreign affairs of the People's Republic of China), vol. 3. Beijing: Shijioe zhishi chubanshe, 1958, p. 62, as cited in Keith, *The Diplomacy of Zhou Enlai*, p, 71.
15. John Foster Dulles' June 1956 Speech at Iowa University, as cited in Norman Graebner, *Cold War Diplomacy 1945–1960*. Princeton: Van Nostrand, 1962, p. 97.
16. 'Premier Chou En-lai's Speech at Banquet', Peking, 20 October 1943, *Survey of China Mainland Press*, no. 912, 20 October 1954, pp. 3–4.
17. Graebner, *Cold War Diplomacy 1945–1960*, p. 87.
18. Zhou Enlai, 'Strengthen Party Unity and Oppose Bourgeois Individualism', (10 February 1954), in *Selected Works of Zhou Enlai*, vol. ii, p. 136.
19. Zhou Enlai, 'Speeches at the Plenary Session of the Asian-African Conference', in *Selected Works of Zhou Enlai*, vol. ii, p. 161.
20. Ibid., p. 163.
21. Ibid., p. 165.
22. Ibid., p. 164.
23. Ronald C. Keith, 'History, Contradiction, and the Apotheosis of Mao Zedong', *China Review International*, vol. 2, no. 1, Spring 2004, p. 2.

24. Mao Tse-tung, 'On the Draft Constitution of the People's Republic of China' (14 June 1954), in *Selected Works of Mao Tse-tung*, vol. v. Peking: Foreign Languages Press, 1977, p. 146.

25. Stuart Schram, ed., *Mao Tse-tung Unrehearsed*, pp. 126, 129, as cited in Ronald C. Keith, 'China's Modernization and the Policy of Self-Reliance', *China Report*, vol. 19, no. 3, March–April 1983, p. 24.

26. Zhou Enlai, 'The Implementation of the First Five-Year Plan' (16 September 1956), in *Selected Works of Zhou Enlai*, vol. ii, pp. 230–1.

27. Mao Tse-tung, 'Speech at the Lushan Plenum' (23 July 1959), in Stuart R. Schram, ed., *Mao Tse-tung Unrehearsed*. Harmondsworth: Penguin Books, 1975, p. 143.

28. Mao Tse-tung, 'On Ten Major Relationships' (25 April 1956), in *The Selected Works of Mao Tse-tung*, vol. v, p. 303.

29. Ibid., p. 303.

30. Ibid., p. 305, author's italics.

31. Mao Zedong, 'A Talk to the Music Workers' (24 August 1956), *Beijing Review*, no. 37, 14 September 1979, p. 13, author's italics.

32. See entry under 'internationalism' in Tom Bottomore, ed., *A Dictionary of Marxist Thought*. Harvard University Press, 1983, p. 232. For the related text see *Marxism-Leninism on Proletarian Internationalism*. Moscow: Progress Publishers, 1972, pp. 177–8.

33. 'Premier Chou En-lai's Press Conference in Cairo', *Afro-Asian Solidarity Against Imperialism*. Peking: Foreign Languages Press, 1964, p. 17.

34. 'Premier Chou En-lai's Speech at the Meeting of Cadres of the Algerian National Liberation Front', *Afro-Asian Solidarity Against Imperialism*, p. 70.

35. Zhou repeated these remarks in his speech over Indonesian radio, 'Premier Zhou Enlai Makes Farewell Speech over Radio Indonesia', NCNC, Djakarta, 25 April, 1965, *Survey of the China Mainland Press*, no. 3447, p. 32.

36. 'Premier Chou En-lai's Press Conference in Mogadiscio', 3 February 1964, *Afro-Asian Solidarity Against Imperialism*, p. 291.

37. For the 'two methods' see 'Premier Chou En-lai's Press Conference in Cairo', p. 17.

38. 'Whence the Differences', *People's Daily*, editorial of 27 February 1963 as carried in the *Peking Review*, no. 9, 1 March 1963, p. 10.

39. Melvin Gurtov and Byong-Moo Hwang, *China Under Threat: The Politics of Strategy and Diplomacy*. Baltimore and London: Johns Hopkins University Press, 1980, p. 203.

40. Ibid., p. 204.

41. Albert Feuerwerker, 'Chinese History and the Foreign Relations of Contemporary China', *The Annals*, AAPSS, July 1972, vol. 402, p. 10.

42. Lin Biao, 'Long Live the Victory of the People's War', in K.H. Fan, *The Chinese Cultural Revolution: Selected Documents*. New York: Grove Press, 1968, p. 94.

43. Allen Whiting, 'The Use of Force in Foreign Policy by the People's Republic of China', *The Annals*, AAPSS, July 1972, vol. 402, p. 55.

44. This repeats the analysis and citations in Ronald C. Keith, 'Mao Zedong and His Political Thought', in Anthony Parel and Ronald C. Keith, eds, *Comparative Philosophy: Studies under the Upas Tree*. Lanham, Boulder, New York and London: Lexington Books, 2003, p. 103.

45. Ronald C. Keith, 'The Origins and Strategic Implications of China's "Independent Foreign Policy"', *International Journal*, vol. xli, no. 1, Winter 1985–86, p. 113.

46. Zao Yingwang, *Zhongguo waijiao diyi ren* (The first person in China's diplomacy). Shanghai: Shanghai renmin chubanshe, 2006, p. 50.

47. Henry Kissinger, *A World Restored*. Boston: Houghton Mifflin Co., 1957, pp. 1–2.

48. Henry Kissinger, *White House Years*. Boston and Toronto: Little, Brown & Co., 1979, p. 781.

49. Ibid., p. 1063.

50. William Burr, ed., *The Kissinger Transcripts*. New York: The Free Press, 1998, p. 181.

51. Henry Kissinger, *Years of Upheaval*. Boston and Toronto: Little, Brown & Co., 1982, p. 50.

52. Keith, 'China's Modernization and the Policy of 'Self-Reliance', p. 21.

53. *Speech by the Chairman of the Delegation of the People's Republic of China, Teng Hsiao-ping, at the Special Session of the UN General Assembly* (10 April 1974). Peking: Foreign Languages Press, 1974, p. 15.

54. Deng Xiaoping, 'The Principles of Peaceful Coexistence Have a Potentially Wide Application' (31 October 1984), in *Selected Works of Deng Xiaoping*, vol. iii (1982–92). Beijing: Foreign Languages Press, 1994, p. 102.

55. Deng Xiaoping, 'For the Great Unity of the Entire Chinese Nation', in *Selected Works of Deng Xiaoping*, vol. iii, p. 165.

56. Wang Congbiao, 'Deng Xiaoping and [the] Shenzhen Economic Zone', Foreign Broadcast Information Service, FBIS-CHI-92-198, 13 October 1993, p. 12.
57. Deng Xiaoping, *Selected Works of Deng Xiaoping*, vol. ii (1975–82). Beijing: Foreign Languages Press, 1984, pp. 263–4.
58. 'Replies to the American TV Correspondent Mike Wallace' (2 September 1986), in *Selected Works of Deng Xiaoping*, vol. iii, p. 176.
59. Deng Xiaoping, 'With Stable Policies of Reform and Opening to the Outside World, China Can Have Great Hopes for the Future' (16 June 1989), in *Selected Works of Deng Xiaoping*, vol. iii, p. 311.
60. Deng Xiaoping, 'With Stable Policies of Reform and Opening', p. 310.
61. Ibid.
62. Zhou Enlai, 'Construction and Unity' (14 August 1950), *Selected Works of Zhou Enlai*, vol. ii. Beijing: Foreign Languages Press, 1989, p. 39.

3   Connecting the 'Rule of Law', 'Human Rights' and 'Democracy' in China

1. 'Constitutionalism and China', in Li Buyun, *Constitutionalism and China (Xianzheng yu Zhongguo)*, translated by Huang Lie. Beijing: Falu chubanshe, 2006, pp. 2–3.
2. *Building of Political Democracy in China*, last page, last paragraph, http://english.people.con.cn/whitepaper/democracy
3. The original source is Deng Xiaoping, 'Reform the Political Structure and Strengthen the People's Sense of Legality', in Deng Xiaoping, *Fundamental Issues in Present Day China*. Beijing: Foreign Languages Press, 1987, p. 145.
4. These four principles include keeping to the socialist road, upholding the democratic dictatorship of the proletariat, the leadership of the CCP and upholding Marxism-Leninism Mao Zedong Thought.
5. Jude Howell, 'Getting to the Roots: Governance Pathologies and Future Prospects', in Jude Howell, ed., *Governance in China*. Lanham, Boulder and New York: Rowman & Littlefield, p. 238.
6. See Yijiang Ding on the changing meaning of 'democracy' and the related issues of civil society versus state corporatism: David Ding, *Democracy since Tiananmen Square*. Vancouver: University of British Columbia Press, 2001, passim; and also Yijiang Ding, 'Corporatism and Civil Society in China: An Overview of the Debate

in Recent Years', *China Information*, vol. xii, no. 4, Spring 1998, pp. 44–67.

7. Ding, *Democracy Since Tiananmen Square*, p. 121.

8. *Zhonghua renmin gongheguo xianfa* (*Constitution of the People's Republic of China*). Beijing: Foreign Languages Press, 2004, p. 19.

9. See Julia Howell comment on Julia Howell, 'Prospects for NGOs in China', *Development in Practice*, vol. 5, no. 1, February 1995, in Ronald C. Keith, Zhiqiu Lin and Huang Lie, 'The Making of a Chinese NGO: The Research and Intervention Project on Domestic Violence', *Problems of Post-Communism*, vol. 50, no. 1, November/December 2003, p. 41.

10. Zhou Tianyong, interviewed on 17 April by Radio86 on 'Storming the Fortress: A Research Report on the Reform of China's Political Institutions after the 17th Party Congress', repeated in the *Beijing Review*.

11. Sun Yatsen, Lecture Three, *San Min Chu Yi*, Frank Price, translated, Shanghai, 1927, p. 80.

12. Kenneth Lieberthal, *Governing China, From Revolution through Reform*. New York: W.W. Norton & Co., 1995. pp. 7–8. Lieberthal discusses how Confucian tradition encouraged certain patterns of speech and conformity of thinking with the prescribed ideas imbedded in the social order.

13. Chang Chih-Tung, *China's Only Hope*, trans. by Samuel Woodbridge. Westport, Conn.: Hyperion Press Inc., pp. 56–7.

14. 'Text of CPC Central Committee Decision on Enhancing Ability to Govern', Xinhua, 16 September 2004, FBIS-CHI-2004-0926, NewsEdge Document No. 200410041477.1-9d5b1b9fd4e2f3fe, p. 2.

15. For discussion, for example, see Pitman Potter, 'Legal Reform in China: Institutions, Culture and Selective Adaptation', *Law and Social Inquiry*, vol. 29, no. 2, 2004, pp. 465–96.

16. 'Conclusion', *Building of Political Democracy*, p. 43.

17. 'China's Efforts and Achievements in Promoting the Rule of Law (1)', Xinhua, 28 February 2008, NewsEdge Document No. 200902281477.1-2ebc26168ccf50093, Foreword, p. 1.

18. For discussion of criminal justice in historical context see R.C. Keith and Zhiqiu Lin, *New Crime in China: Public Order and Human Rights*. London and New York: Routledge (Taylor & Francis), 2005, pp. 8–9.

19. Deng Xiaoping's Speech to the Third Plenum of the Eleventh Central Committee on 13 December 1978 as cited and discussed in Ronald C. Keith, *China's Struggle for the Rule of Law*. New York: St Martin's Press, 1994, p. 9.

20. This statement in the Party's own leading journal, *Hongqi* (Red Flag), is analysed in Keith, *China's Struggle for the Rule of Law*, p. 13.
21. Article Five, *Zhonghua renmin gongheguo xianfa* (Constitution of the People's Republic of China). Beijing: Foreign Languages Press, 2004, p. 21.
22. Deng Xiaoping, 'Help the People Understand the Rule of Law' (28 June 1986), in *Selected Works of Deng Xiaoping*, vol. iii. Beijing: Foreign Languages Press, 1994, p. 166.
23. As cited and discussed in Keith, *China's Struggle for the Rule of Law*, p. 120.
24. Keith and Lin, *New Crime in China*, p. 14.
25. Last Paragraph, Preamble, Party Constitution, 1992. For a convenient text refer to Constitution of the Communist Party 14 November 2002, in Documents of the 16th National Congress of the Communist Party of China. Beijing: Foreign Languages Press, 2002, pp. 86–7.
26. See Chih-yu Shih on this point, 'Contending Theories of "Human Rights with Chinese Characteristics"', *Issues and Studies*, vol. 29, no. 11, November 1993, pp. 58–9.
27. Keith, *China's Struggle for the Rule of Law*, p. 43.
28. Louis Henkin, 'Confucianism, Human Rights, and "Cultural Relativism"', in William Theodore de Bary and Tu Weiming, eds, *Confucianism and Human Rights*. New York: Columbia University Press, 1998, pp. 311–12.
29. Deng Xiaoping, 'China Will Never Allow Other Countries to Interfere in its Internal Affairs' (11 July 1990), in *Selected Works of Deng Xiaoping*, vol. iii, p. 347.
30. Ibid., p. 348.
31. Keith, *China's Struggle for the Rule of Law*, p. 55.
32. Information Office, State Council, 'A Report Which Distorts Facts and Confuses Right and Wrong', *Beijing Review*, 13–19 March 1995, p. 21.
33. Information Office, State Council, 'Human Rights in China', November 1991, *Beijing Review*, 4–10 November 1991, *Beijing Review*, 13–19 March 1995, p. 21.
34. Information Office, State Council, 'Human Rights in China', *Beijing Review*, 4–10 November 1991, p. 45.
35. Li Lin, 'Quanqiuhua beijihngxide Zhongguo lifa fazhan' (China's legislative development in the globalization context) in *Falixue, fashixue* (Jurisprudence and Legal History), no. 3, 1998, p. 31, as cited in Ronald C. Keith, '"Internationalization" and "Localization" in the Chinese Search for Human Justice', in Sheeren Ismael, ed., *Globalization: Policies, Challenges and Responses*. Calgary: Detslig, 1999, p. 143.

36. NPC Legal Work Committee, *Zhonghua renmin gongheguo jiehunfa: xiugai lifa ziliaoxuan* (The Marriage Law of the People's Republic of China: Selected Legislative Materials). Beijing: Falu chubanshe, 2002.
37. Keith and Lin, *New Crime in China*, pp. 76–7.
38. Keith, Lin and Lie, 'The Making of a Chinese NGO', p. 48.
39. Information Office, State Council, *Progress in China's Human Rights Cause in 2000*. Beijing: Foreign Languages Press, 2001, p. 14.
40. 'Progress in China's Human Rights Cause in 2003', Information Office, State Council, *White Papers of the Chinese Government* (English and Chinese), pp. 412–13 in English.
41. 'Shiyijie quanguo renda jihua weilai wunian lifa 64jian' (The Eleventh NPC plan for 64 items of legislation), CCTV, 29 October 2008, 13:23.
42. Keith and Lin, *New Crime in China*, p. 27.
43. Bruce Gilley, *China's Democratic Future*. New York: Columbia University Press, 2004, p. xiii.
44. Robert Compton, *East Asian Democratization: Impact of Globalization, Culture and Economy*. West Port, Conn. and London: Praeger, 2000.
45. Larry Diamond, *Developing Democracy: Toward Consolidation*. Baltimore and London: Johns Hopkins University Press, 1999, pp. 167–8.
46. Larry Diamond and Marc Plattner, eds, *Democracy in East Asia*. Baltimore: Johns Hopkins University Press, 1998, p. xxviii.
47. Yu Xinyan, 'Basic Differences between Socialist Democracy and Capitalist Democracy', *Beijing ribao*, 22 October 1989, in FBIS-CH(-89-206), 16 October 1989, p. 16.
48. Ibid., p. 17.
49. Ibid., p. 18.
50. *Building of Political Democracy in China*, Section 1, p. 2. http://english.people.com.cn/whitepaper/democracy/dem
51. Ibid., Section 1, pp. 5–6.
52. 'Text of CPC Central Committee Decision on Enhancing Ability to Govern', Xinhua, 26 September 2004, NewsEdge Document No. 299410041477.1_9d5b1bfd4e2f3fe, 2nd of 18 pages.
53. *Building of Political Democracy in China*, 2005, Section 2, p. 3 of 3.
54. See section on 'Government Democracy', in *Building of Political Democracy in China*, 2005, 2nd of 5 pages in this section.
55. Section 9, 'Government Democracy', in *Building of Political Democracy in China*, 3rd of 5 pages.

56. Brantly Womack, 'Democracy and the Governing Party: A Theoretical Perspective', *Journal of Chinese Political Science*, vol. 10, no. 1, April 2005, passim.
57. Hu Jintao, 'Hold High the Great Banner of Socialism with Chinese Characteristics and Strive for New Victories in Building a Moderately Prosperous Society in all Respects', in *Documents of the 17th National Congress of the Communist Party of China*. Beijing: Foreign Languages Press, 2007, p. 36.
58. He Chunzhong, 'Li Junru Stresses Economic, Political Structural Reforms Go Hand in Hand', *Zhongguo Wangnian bao*, 21 April 2008, NewsEdge Document No. 200804211477.1_469a2f7d1f7c8fdb, p. 7 of 10 pages.
59. Ibid., p. 8.
60. David Shambaugh, *China's Communist Party: Atrophy and Adaptation*. University of California Press, 2008, p. 175.
61. The problem of the fair assessment of China is addressed in Randall Peerenboom, 'Assessing Human Rights in China: Why the Double Standard?', *Cornell International Law Journal*, vol. 38, no. 1, 2005, pp. 71–170.
62. Arch Puddington, 'The 2007 Freedom House Survey: Is the Tide Turning?', *Journal of Democracy*, vol. 19, no. 2, April 2008, p. 64, and Larry Diamond, 'The Democratic Rollback: The Resurgence of the Predatory State', *Foreign Affairs*, vol. 87, no. 2, March–April 2008, pp. 36–7.
63. Jonathan Hecht, 'Can Legal Reform Roster Respect for Human Rights in China?', 11 April 2002 Testimony Before the Congressional Executive Commission on China, p. 2.
64. 'Text of CPC Central Committee Decision on Enhancing the Ability to Govern', Xinhua, 26 September 2004, NewsEdge Document No. 2004100414771.1_9d5b1b9fd4e2f3f3, p. 2 of 18.
65. See He Baogang, *The Democratization of China*. London and New York: Routledge, 1996, p. 52. He refers to Deng's model of democracy as a 'formalistic democracy' that only served to justify 'paternalistic power rather than a means of public control over government'.
66. Hu Jintao, 'Hold High the Great Banner of Socialism', pp. 16–17.

4 'Socialism', or 'Capitalism with Chinese Characteristics'?

1. Deng Xiaoping, 'Opening Speech at the Twelfth National Congress of the Communist Party of China', in *Selected Works of Deng Xiaoping*, vol. iii. Beijing: Foreign Languages Press, 1994, p. 14.

2. Deng Xiaoping, 'We Shall Concentrate on Economic Development', (18 September 1982), *Selected Works*, vol. iii, p. 21.

3. 'Journal on Deng in Shenzhen Special Zone', FBIS-CHI-82-198, 13 October 1992, p. 17.

4. Deng Xiaoping, 'Excerpts from Talks Given in Wuchang, Shanzhen, Zhuhai and Shanghai' (18 January–21 February, 1992), *Selected Works*, vol. iii, p. 369.

5. Chinese Communist Party, *Resolution on CCP History (1949–1981)*. Beijing: Foreign Languages Press, 1981.

6. 'On the General Program of Work for the Whole Party and the Whole Nation', in Chi Hsin, *The Case of the Gang of Four*. Hong Kong: Cosmos Books Inc. and Books New China, Inc., 1977, p. 223.

7. Deng Xiaoping, 'Let the Facts Speak for themselves', *Selected Works*, vol. iii, p. 199.

8. Deng Xiaoping, 'Remarks at the Sixth Plenary Session of the Party's Twelfth Central Committee' (28 September 1986), *Selected Works*, vol. iii, pp. 182–3.

9. Deng Xiaoping, 'Replies to the American TV Correspondent Make Wallace', *Selected Works*, vol. iii, p. 174.

10. Deng Xiaoping, 'Take A Clear-cut Stand against Bourgeois Liberalization' (30 December 1986), *Selected Works*, vol. iii, pp. 194, 197.

11. Deng Xiaoping, 'Address to Officers at the Rank of General and Above in Command of the Troops Enforcing Martial Law in Beijing' (9 June 1989), *Selected Works*, vol. iii, p. 295.

12. Ibid., p. 298.

13. Ibid., p. 299.

14. Deng Xiaoping, 'Exceprts from Talks Given in Wuchang, Shenzhen, Zhuhai and Shanghai' (18 January–21 February 1992), *Selected Works*, vol. iii, p. 358.

15. Ibid., p. 360.

16. Ibid., p. 361.

17. 'Decision of the CPC Central Committee on Some Issues Concerning the Establishment of a Socialist Market Economic Structure', *Beijing Review*, 22–28 November 1993, author's italics.

18. Deng Xiaoping, 'Seize the Opportunity to Develop the Economy', *Selected Works*, vol. iii, p. 351.

19. See Ronald C. Keith and Zhiqiu Lin, *Law and Justice in China's New Marketplace*. London: Palgrave, 2001, p. 15.

20. 'Decision of the CPC on Some Issues Concerning the Establishment of a Socialist Market Economic Structure', *Beijing Review*, 22–28 November 1993, p. 18.

21. Wang Weiguang covered the meeting in a key editorial 'Correctly Understand and Handle Conflicts of Interests Among the People in the New Period'. *Renmin ribao* (People's Daily), 22 June 1999.
22. Jiang Zemin, 'Hold High the Great Banner of Deng Xiaoping Theory for an All-round Advancement of the Cause of Building Socialism with Chinese Characteristics into the 21st Century', *Beijing Review*, 6–12 October 1997, p. 20.
23. Ibid., pp. 12–16.
24. Report in *Beijing Review*, 6–12 October 1997, p. 14.
25. *Zhonghua renmin gongheguo xianfa*, 2004, p. 111, author's italics.
26. Ibid., p. 113, author's italics.
27. Jiang Zemin, '"Three Represents" Is the Essence of the Existence of our Party, the Foundation of Ruling Power, and the Fountainhead of our Strength' (14 May 2000), in *On the 'Three Represents'*. Beijing: Foreign Languages Press, 2001.
28. Willy Wo-Lap Lam, 'The Communist Party vs. Peasants and Workers: Will Hu Jintao's "New Social Contract" Work?', in Willy Wo-Lap Lam, *Chinese Politics in the Hu Jintao Era: New Leaders, New Challenges*. Armonk and London: M.E. Sharpe, 2006, pp. 63–106.
29. Jiang Zemin, *On the 'Three Represents'*, p. 36.
30. 'CPC Central Committee Decision on Enhancing the Party's Ability to Govern', Xinhua, 26 September 2004, NewsEdge Document No. 200410041477.1-9d5b1b9fd4e2f3fe, p. 6.
31. Keith and Lin, *Law and Justice in China's New Marketplace*, p. 144.
32. Amended Article 11, *Constitution of the People's Republic of China* (Zhonghua renmin gongheguo xianfa). Beijing: Zhongguo fazhi chubanshe, 2001, p. 119.
33. The *White Paper on the PRC's Efforts in Promoting the Rule of Law*. On p. 5 it is noted that there were seven rounds on this vital issue. The White Paper claimed that such extended debate confirmed China's commitment to democracy.
34. Chen Yongjie, 'Central Party School Professor Lin dong Says Opposition to Law on Property Rights Lacks Legal Principle', 3 March 2007, *Mingbao*, Hong Kong, NewsEdge Document No. 200703031477.1_797b0198df837ac.
35. Peter Ho, 'Who Owns China's Land? Policies, Rights and Deliberate Institutional Ambiguity', *China Quarterly*, no. 166, June 2001, p. 400.

36. 'Civil Resistance and Rule of Law in China', in Perry and Goldman, eds, *Grassroots Political Reform in Contemporary China*. Cambridge, Mass.: Harvard University Press, 2007, p. 194.

37. 'Property Legislation Embodies Spirit and Principle of Constitution', 10 March 2007, NewsEdge Document No. 200703101477.1_ fb6b0100b3aeba4e: *Renmin ribao* online.

38. 'Property Law May Serve as Umbrella to Farmers' Land: Chinese Lawmaker', Xinhua, 8 March 2007, NewsEdge Document No. 200703081477.1-6ecb00584c5ea1e2.

39. James Dorn, 'Ownership with Chinese Characteristics: Private Property Rights and Land Reform in the PRC', 3 February 2003 Testimony to the Congressional-Executive Commission on China Issues roundtable, http:///www.cato.org/testimony/ct-jd02032003. html

40. Wang Zhaoguo, 'Explanation on the Draft Property Law of the People's Republic of China', 8 March 2007, NewsEdge Document No. 200703081477.1_8ca512b7cbaf351d, p. 5.

41. Yongshun Cai, 'Civil Resistance and the Rule of Law in China', in Perry and Goldman, *Grassroots Political Reform in Contemporary China*, p. 190.

42. Chinese politics is increasingly witnessing the development of 'righteous resistance'. See Kevin O'Brien, *Rightful Resistance in Rural China*. Cambridge: Cambridge University Press, 2006, pp. 1–24.

43. Zhang Rui, 'First Test Case for Newly Approved Property Law?', *Zhongguo Wang*, 24 March 2007, china.org.cn in NewsEdge Document No. 200703241477.1_02eb00eb9208b41f.

44. 'Chongqing Property-Owning Couple Put up Lone Fight Against Developer', *Ming Pao*, 26 March 2007, NewsEdge Document No. 200703261477.1_9f70027250253b59).

45. 'CPC Central Committee Decision on Enhancing the Party's Ability to Govern', 24 September 2004, NewsEdge Document No. 200410041477.1_9d5b1b9fd4e2f3fe, p. 6.

46. 'Hu: Harmonious Society Crucial for Progress' (30 June 2005), http:/www.chiaembassyl.org.nz/eng/xw/t201713.htm.

5 China's New 'Model' of International Relations

1. Deng Xiaoping, 'We Must Unite the People on the Basis of Firm Convictions' (9 November 1986), in *Selected Works of Deng Xiaoping*, vol. iii. Beijing: Foreign Languages Press, 1994, p. 191.

2. Deng's related 24-character instruction formed the basis of China's foreign policy response to the anti-Tiananmen Square position of Western countries: 'Observe developments soberly, maintain our

position, meet challenges calmly, hide our capacities and bide our time remaining free of ambition and never claiming leadership.' Realists have focused on 'hide our capacities' as indicative of a grand strategy of deception. 'Never claim leadership' particularly concerns the post-Tiananmen contradictions in Sino-US relations. See Guan Li, *Deng Xiaoping yu Meiguo* (Deng Xiaoping and the United States). Beijing: Zhonggongdangshi chubanshe, 2004, p. 606. Also see Rosemary Foot, 'Chinese Strategies in a US-Hegemonic Global Order: Accommodating and Hedging', *International Affairs*, vol. 82, no. 1, 2006, p. 84.

3. 'China's Peaceful Development Road' (December 2005), p. 1. Available from http://www.china.org.cn/english/2005/Dec/152669. htm

4. Ye Zicheng, *Xin Zhongguo waijiao sixiang cong Mao Zedong dao Deng Xiaoping* (New Chinese Diplomatic Thought from Mao Zedong to Deng Xiaoping). Beijing: Beijing daxue chubanshe, 2001, p. 423.

5. Lu Hong, 'Work Together to Build a Harmonious World (International Forum)', *Renmin ribao* (People's Daily), 13 May 2005, NewsEdge Document No. 200505131477.1_9c5600c51359538c, author's italics.

6. For related comment on 'rising' see Chu Shulong and Jin Wei, *Zhongguo waijiao zhanlue he zhengce* (China's Foreign Strategy and Policy). Beijing: Shishi chubanshe, 2008, p. 112. For the ups and downs of 'peaceful rise' see Bonnie S. Glaser and Evan Mederos, 'The Changing Ecology of Foreign-Policy Making in China: The Ascension and Demise of the Theory of "Peaceful Rise"', *China Quarterly*, vol. 190 (June 2007), pp. 291–310.

7. Chu Shulong and Jin Wei, *Zhongguo waijiao zhanlue*, p. 48.

8. For discussion of the connotations and origins of 'independent foreign policy' see Ronald C. Keith, 'The Origins and Strategic Implications of China's "Independent Foreign Policy"', *International Journal*, vol. xli, no. 1, Winter (1985–86), pp. 95–128.

9. Hu Jintao at CPC Central Committee Political Bureau's 10th Collective Study Session...', Xinhua, 24 February 2004, NewsEdge Document No. 20040222511477.1_6553003a5e310086x.

10. Foot, 'Chinese Strategies in a US-Hegemonic Global Order', pp. 85–7.

11. Joshua Cooper Ramo, *The Beijing Consensus: Notes on the New Physics of Chinese Power*. London: The Foreign Policy Centre, p. 1. The title refers to New Physics, but the Introduction refers to new math.

12. Hu Jintao, 'Hold High the Great Banner of Socialism with Chinese Characteristics and Strive for New Victories in Building a Moderately Prosperous Society in All Respects', 15 October 2007 report to the 17th National Congress of the Communist Party of China, in *Documents of the 17th National Congress of the Communist Party of China*. Beijing: Foreign Languages Press, 2007, p. 25.

13. For related gloss on 'seek the truth from the facts' see Ronald C. Keith, 'Mao Zedong and his Political Thought', in Anthony Parel and Ronald C. Keith, eds, *Comparative Political Philosophy*, second edition. Lanham: Lexington Books, 2003, p. 104.

14. Hu's harmony is related to the incised aphorism on the wall of the New York UN building, 'Do not do unto others what you would not want done unto you.' Li Zhaoxing, 'Peace, Development and Cooperation-Banner for China's Diplomacy in the New Era', Xinhua, 22 August 2005, cgubanuk,cin,cb/site1/xwp.dxw/2005-08/23/content-278277.htm

15. Professor Li is cited in 'PRC FM Li Zhaoxing: Ancient Philosophy Guides China's Modern Diplomacy of Harmony', Xinhua, 5 September 2003, NewsEdge Document. No. 200509051477.1_eced600830ef80892.

16. 'Wen Jiabao Delivers Speech Marking Five Principles of Peaceful Coexistence Anniversary', Xinhua, 28 June 2004, p. 3, NewsEdge Document No. 200406291477.1_12b001a0edd6e34a, author's italics.

17. Xiong Guangkai, 'An Epoch-making Conference, a Powerful Trans-Century Voice', *Guoji xingshi yu anquan zhanlue* (International Situation and Security Strategy). Beijing: Qinghua daxue chubanshe, 2006, p. 273. General Xiong also elaborates on the '*he*' character in a second speech in the same volume, 'For Common Security in a Harmonious Asia-Pacific', p. 308.

18. 'Wen Jiabao Delivers Speech Marking Five Principles', p. 2.

19. Ronald C. Keith, *The Diplomacy of Zhou Enlai*. London: Macmillan, 1989, p. 2. For a comment on Nehruvian diplomacy's representation of India as a civilization see Amitra Narlikar, 'Peculiar Chauvinism or Strategic Calculation? Explaining the Negotiating Strategy of a Rising India', *International Affairs*, vol. 82, no. 21, 2006, p. 72.

20. 'RMRB Article Views Global Popularity of Confucius, China's Peaceful Rise', *Renmin ribao* (People's Daily), 29 September 2005, NewsEdge Document No. 200509291477.1_81f600bc65024ac0.

21. Ibid.

22. 'Xiong Guangkai's Article Says PRC's Development, Peaceful, Open and Cooperative', Xinhua, 28 December 2005, NewsEdge Document No. 200512281477.1_10ce00b009feb426.

23. Hu Jintao, 'Strive to Build a Harmonious World Where There Are Permanent Peace and Prosperity', speech at the 60th anniversary of the UN, 15 September 2005, Xinhua, 16 September 2005, NewsEdge Document No. 200509161477.1_4eb805b96f4909f9c, p. 4, author's italics.

24. Ronald C. Keith, 'The post-Cold War Symmetry of Russo-Chinese Bilateralism', *International Journal*, vol. xlix, no. 4 (Autumn 1994), p. 770.

25. Ibid., p. 771.

26. Ibid., p. 775.

27. For example of such analysis see Su Hao, *Cong yaling dao ganlan: Ya-Tai hezuo anquan yanjiu* (From Muscular [Diplomacy] to Olive Branch: Studies in Asian Pacific Security Cooperation). Beijing: Shijie zhishi chubanshe, 2003, pp. 64–6.

28. Xiong Guangkai, 'Promote "Shanghai Spirit" and Boost Peace and Development', *International Strategic Studies*, Beijing, no. 4, (October 2004), pp. 2–3, author's italics.

29. The Five Principles of Peaceful Coexistence: What is There to Learn 50 Years Later?', *Beijing Review*, vol. 47, no. 23 (10 June 2004), p. 18.

30. 'China's Peaceful Development Road', (December 2005). Available from http://www.china.org.cn/english/2005/Dec/152669.htm, p. 2.

31. Wen Jiabao, 'A Number of Issues Regarding the Historic Tasks in the Initial Stage of Socialism and China's Foreign Policy', Xinhua, 26 February 2007, NewsEdge Document No. 200702261477.1-021d0a66834796f4, p. 3.

32. Mearsheimer disparaged 'folks' who travel to Beijing to meet 'X, Y and Z' and come back saying 'China can rise peacefully.' Panel: China, the United States and the World, at the 28–29 April 2006 Chicago Conference, 'China and the Future of the World', p. 9, author's italics. http://chicagosociety.edu/china/coverage.htm

33. Ibid., p. 16.

34. In his discussion of China's 'grand strategy', Goldstein suggests that the Chinese have seen the US 'China Threat' as 'the East Asian facet' of a US strategy to 'sow divisions [among the region's states and]…to prevent China from becoming developed and powerful'. See Avery Goldstein, 'The Diplomatic Fact of China's Grand Strategy: A Rising Power's Emerging Choice', *China Quarterly*, no. 168 (December 2001), p. 840. On p. 842, Goldstein argues that since the early 1990s China has increased its level of international activism and that the latter is characterized by the rejection of traditional diplomatic strategy based on alliance formation, partnership with major powers as well as active multilateralism.

35. Hu Jintao, 'Lasting Peace and Common Prosperity', UN, 60th Session, 15 September 2005. Available from http://1b2.mofcom. gov.cn/article/chinanews/200511/2991100766747.html
36. 'China's Peaceful Development Road', p. 2.
37. Marc Lanteigne, 'The Developmentalism/Globalization Conundrum in Chinese Governance', in Andre Laliberte and Marc Lanteigne, eds, *The Chinese Party-State in the 21st Century*. London and New York: Routledge/Taylor Francis Group, 2007, p. 163. For related gloss on the Chinese concept of 'globalization' see R. Keith, ed., *China as a Rising World Power and its Response to 'Globalization'*. London and New York: Routledge Taylor & Francis, 2005), pp. 6–8.
38. Wen Jiabao, 'Our Historical Tasks at the Primary Stage of Socialism and Several Issues Concerning China's Foreign Policy', Xinhua, 26 February 2007, NewsEdge Document No. 200702261477.1-021d0a66834796f4, p. 4.
39. Hu Jintao, 'Hold High the Great Banner of Socialism with Chinese Characteristics and Strive for New Victories...', Report to the 17th National Congress of the Chinese Communist Party. Available from http://en.chinaelections.org/newsinfo.asp?newsid=12146, p. 37, author's italics.
40. See the third lecture in Sun Yatsen (Frank Price trans., L.T. Chen, ed.), *San Min Chu I* (The Three People's Principles) in English and Chinese texts. Shanghai: China Committee, Institute of Pacific Relations, 1927, pp. 14–16.
41. Yang Jiechi, for example, used this expression. See 'Address by Chinese Foreign Minister Yang Jiechi at the 14th ARF Foreign Minister's Meeting', Manila, 2 August 2007.

6 China Redux?

1. 'Chairman Mao's Talk to the Music Workers' (24 August 1956) was one of the several items that Deng circulated in his introduction of new reform strategy. As reproduced in *Beijing Review*, no. 37, 14 September 1979, pp. 9–14.
2. Section 1, 'A Choice Suited to China's Conditions', Information Office, State Council, *Building of Political Democracy in China*, p. 5 of section's six pages, author's italics.
3. *Speech by the Chairman of the Delegation of the People's Republic of China, Teng Hsiao-ping, at the Special Session of the UN General Assembly* (10 April 1974). Peking: Foreign Languages Press, 1974, p. 15.
4. See the *Renmin ribao* (People's Daily) analysis, 'Unswervingly Take the Road of Peaceful Development', 2 September 2005, Xinhua,

NewsEdge Document No. 200509211477.1_497a02d11bbc4eb8, pp. 1–2.

5. Deng Xiaoping, 'Make a Success of Special Economic Zones and Open More Cities to the Outside World' (24 February 1984), in *Selected Works of Deng Xiaoping*, vol. iii. Beijing: Foreign Languages Press, 1994, pp. 61–2.

6. Luo Renshi, 'Defense for Common Security', *International Strategic Studies*, no. 1, 2001, p. 23, in Ronald C. Keith, 'The Chinese "New Security Concept": The Revolution in Military Affairs, Space Weaponization and Prospective Arms Control Cooperation', published paper prepared for International Security Bureau, International Security Research and Outreach Programme, Canadian Department of Foreign Affairs and International Trade, December 2002, Ottawa, p. 10.

7. Li Zhongjie, 'Our Country Needs an International Strategy at a Higher Level – Part Eight on How to Understand and Approach the Current International Strategic Situation', *Liaowang*, 2 August 2002, in FBIS-CHI-2002-0813, as discussed in Ronald C. Keith, ed., *China as a Rising World Power and its Response to 'Globalization'*. London and New York: Routledge (Taylor & Francis), 2005, pp. 3–4, author's italics.

8. Stuart Schram discusses Mao and the *yin-yang* dialectic in Schram, 'The Marxist', in Dick Wilson, ed., *Mao Tse-tung in the Scales of History*. Cambridge, London, New York, Melbourne: Cambridge University Press, 1977, pp. 60–1.

9. Klaus Mehnert, 'Mao and Maoism: Some Soviet Views', *Current Scene*, vol. viii, no. 15, 1 September 1970, p. 8.

10. Deng Xiaoping, 'Let US Put the Past Behind Us and Open Up a New Era', in *Selected Works of Deng Xiaoping*, vol. iii, p. 284.

11. See, John K. Fairbank, Edwin Reischauer and Albert Craig, *East Asia: The Modern Transformation*. Boston: Houghton Mifflin, 1965, p. 124.

12. Deng Xiaoping, 'Talks in Wuchang, Shenzhen and Shanghai', in *Selected Works of Deng Xiaoping*, vol. iii, p. 368.

SELECTED CONCEPTS IN PINYIN AND CHINESE CHARACTERS

adjustment of interests   *quanli tiaozheng*   管理调整

all-the-people-speak temple   *qun yan tang*   群言堂

China Threat   *Zhongguo weixie*   中国威胁

Chinese characteristics   *Zhongguo tesede*   中国特色的

Chinese learning as substance, Western learning for use   *Zhongxue wei ti, xixue wei yong*   中学为体、西学为用

citizens' rights   *gongmin quan*   公民权

civil society   *shimin shehui*   市民社会

class struggle as the key link   *yi jieji douzheng wei gang*   以阶级斗争为纲

collective peace   *jiti heping*   集体和平

comprehensive management of public order   *shehui zhi-an zonghe zhili*   社会治安综合治理

constitutionalism   *xianzheng*   宪政

cosmopolitanism (also globalism)   *shijiezhuyi*   世界主义

cultivate the self, regulate the family, rule the kingdom and there will be peace under heaven   *xiu shen, qi jia, zhi guo, tianxia ping*   修身、齐家、治国、天下平

cultivating the self   *xiu shen*   修身

custody for repatriation   *shourong qiansong*   收容遣送

decide first, trial later   *xianding, houshen*   先定后审

democratization of international relations   *guoji guanxide minzhu hua*   国际关系的民主化

diplomatic thought   *waijiao sixiang*   外交思想

domestic violence   *jiating baoli*   家庭暴力

efficiency is primary and fairness is supplementary   *xiaoyi wei zhu, gongzheng weifu*   效益为主，公正为辅

Everything Chinese is best   *guocuizhuyi*   国粹主义

extreme heresy   *danibudao*   大逆不道

facing modernization, facing the world, and facing the future   *mianxiang xiandaihua, mianxiang shijie, mianxiang weilai*   面向现代化，面向世界，面向未来

with filial piety rule all under heaven   *yi xiao zhi tianxia*   以孝治天下

five principles of peaceful coexistence   *heping gongchu wuxiang yuanze*   和平共处五项原则

four cardinal principles   *sixiang jiben yuanze*   四项基本原则
four freedoms   *sida ziyou*   四大自由
good government relies on man   *weizheng zai ren*   为政在人
great democracy   *daminzhu*   大民主
Great Han chauvinism   *da Zhonghuazhuyi*   大中华主义
Great Helmsman   *da duoshou*   大舵手
groping the stones on the river bed   *mozhe shitou guohe*
   摸着石头过河
harmonious development   *hexie fazhan*   和谐发展
harmony without uniformity   *he er butong*   和而不统
hegemony   *baquanzhuyi*   霸权主义
human rights   *renquan*   人权
human rights diplomacy   *renquan waijiao*   人权外交
internationalization   *guojihua*   国际化
judicial democracy   *minzhu sifa*   民主司法
know yourself and know your enemy   *zhi ji zhi bi*   知己知彼
the lawful private property of citizens shall not be encroached
   upon   *Gongminde hefade siyou caichan bushou qinfan*
   公民的合法的私有财产不受侵犯。
leaning to one side   *yibian dao*   一边倒
liberate   *jiefang*   解放
localization   *bentuhua*   本土化
the market economy is the rule of law economy   *Shichang jingji shi*
   fazhide jingji   市场经济是法制的经济
Middle Kingdom   *Zhongguo*   中国
mutual security   *xianghu anquan*   相互安全
new security concept   *xin anquan guan*   新安全观
one person temple   *yi yan tang*   一言堂
ownership rights   *suoyou quan*   所有权
past to serve the present   *yigu wei jin*   以古为今
peace and development   *heping yu fazhan*   和平与发展
peaceful rise   *heping jueqi*   和平崛起
policy is the soul of law   *zhengce shi falude linghun*
   政策是法律的灵魂
political-legal system   *zhengfa xitong*   政法系统
pragmatism   *shiyongzhuyi*   实用主义
proceeding from reality in all things   *yi qie cong shiji chufa*
   一切从实际出发
property rights   *caichan quan*   财产权
revisit the past and know new things   *wen gu er zhi xin*   温故而知新
rights and interests   *quanyi*   权益
right of use   *shiyong quan*   使用权
ritual enters law   *li ru yu fa*   礼入于法

rule of law   *fazhi*   法治

rule of man   *renzhi*   人治

ruling party   *zhizheng dang*   执政党

running the country according to law and establishing a socialist rule-of-law country   *yifa zhi guo, jianshe shehuizhuyi fazhi guojia*   依法治国，建设社会主义法治国家

scientific development concept   *kexue fazhan guan*   科学发展观

seek common ground while reserving differences   *qiu tong cunyi*   求同存异。

seek the truth from the facts   *shishi qiu shi*   实事求是

self-reliance   *zili gengsheng*   自力更生

sinification of Marxism-Leninism   *Zhongguohuade MakesiLieningzhuyi*   中国化的马克思列宁主义

study and live until the day that you die   *huodao lao, xuedao lao*   活到老，学到老

study, study and study some more   *xuexi, xuexi, zai xuexi*   学习、学习、再学习

substituting party discipline for the laws of the state   *yi dangji daiti guofa*   以党纪代替国法

superior man is not a utensil   *junzi buqi*   君子不器

theory of productive forces   *shengchanli lilun*   生产力理论

three favourable directions   *sange youli yu*   三个有利于

three privates, one guarantee   *sanzi yibao*   三自一包

three represents   *sange daibiao*   三个代表

unity of theory and practice   *lilun he shiji tongyi*   理论和实际统一

SELECTED READINGS BY CHAPTER THEMES

Historical Perspectives

Buck, Pearl S., *China As I See It*. New York: John Day Co., 1970.

Chang Chih-tung (Zhang Zhidong), *China's Only Hope*, trans. Samuel Woodbridge. Westport, Conn.: Hyperion Press, Inc.

Chen, Jerome, *China and the West: Society and Culture 1815–1937*. London: Hutchinson & Co., 1979.

Chiang, May-Ling Soong, *China Shall Rise Again*. New York and London: Harper Brothers Publishers, c.1941.

China Accuses! Speeches of the Special Representative of the Central People's Government of the People's Republic of China at the United Nations. Beijing: Foreign Languages Press, 1951.

Fairbank, John K., ed., *Chinese Thought and Institutions*. Chicago and London: University of Chicago Press, 1967.

Fairbank, John L. and Edwin O. Reischauer, Albert Craig, *East Asia: Tradition and Transformation*. Boston: Houghton Mifflin Co., 1978.

Goodnow, Frank, *China an Analysis*. New York: Arno Press, 1979, reprint of Johns Hopkins University Press, 1926.

Hunter, Robert and Forrest Davis, *The Red China Lobby*. New York: Fleet Publishing Corporation, 1968.

Koen, Ross Y., *The China Lobby in American Politics*. New York: Harper & Row, 1979.

Rattenbury, Harold B., *Understanding China*. London: Frederick Mueller Ltd, 1942.

Rozman, Gilbert, ed., *The East Asian Region: Confucian Heritage and its Modern Adaptation*. Princeton, N.J.: Princeton University Press, 1991.

Shirokauer, Conrad and Donald N. Clark, *Modern East Asia: A Brief History*. Boston and New York: Houghton Mifflin Co., 2008.

Sun Yatsen, *Sanminzhuyi* (The Three Peoples's Principles), trans. Frank Price, ed. L.T. Chen. Shanghai: Institute of Pacific Relations, 1927, Taipei, 1953 reprint.

Teng Ssu-yu and John K. Fairbank, *China's Response to the West: A Documentary Survey 1839–1923*. New York: Atheneum, 1975.

Terrill, Ross, *The New Chinese Empire and What It Means for the United States*. New York: Basic Books, 2003.

Tsou Rung (Zou Rong), *The Revolutionary Army*, trans. John Lust. The Hague and Paris: L. Mouton & Co., 1968, reprint of 1903 original.

Fitting China into the World

Afro-Asian Solidarity Against Imperialism: A Collection of Documents, Speeches and Press Interviews from the Visits of Chinese Leaders to Thirteen African and Asian Countries. Beijing: Foreign Languages Press, 1964.

Burr, William, ed., *The Kissinger Transcripts*. New York: The Free Press, 1998.

Chen, King C., *China and the Three Worlds: A Foreign Policy Reader*. White Plains, N.Y.: M.W. Sharpe, 1979.

Deng Xiaoping (Teng Hsiaping), *Speech by the Chairman of the Delegation of the People's Republic of China, Teng Hsiao-ping, at the Special Session of the UN General Assembly* (10 April 1974). Peking: Foreign Languages Press, 1974.

Gurtov, Melvin and Byong-Moo Hwang, *China Under Threat: The Politics of Strategy and Diplomacy*. Baltimore and London: Johns Hopkins University Press, 1980.

Keith, Ronald C., 'China's Modernization and the Policy of "Self-Reliance"', *China Report*, vol. xix, no. 2, March–April 1983, pp. 19–34.

Keith, Ronald C., *The Diplomacy of Zhou Enlai*. New York and London: St Martin's Press and Macmillan Press, 1989.

Kissinger, Henry, *White House Years*. Boston and Toronto: Little, Brown & Co., 1970.

Kissinger, Henry, *Years of Upheaval*. Boston and Toronto: Little, Brown & Co., 1982.

Mao Zedong, *The Selected Works of Mao Zedong*, vol. v. Beijing: Foreign Languages Press, 1977.

Margaret Macmillan, *Seize the Hour: When Nixon Met Mao*. London: John Murray, 2007.

Mosher, Steven, *China's Plan to Dominate Asia and the World*. San Francisco: Encounter Books, 2000.

Schram, Stuart, ed., *Mao Tse-tung Unrehearsed*. Harmondsworth: Penguin Books, 1975.

Zhou Enlai, *Selected Works of Zhou Enlai*, vol. ii. Beijing: Foreign Languages Press, 1989.

The Rule of Law, Democracy and Human Rights

Angle, Stephen C. and Marian Svensson, eds, *The Chinese Human Rights Reader: Documents and Commentary 1900–2000*. Armonk and London: M.E. Sharpe, 2001.

De Bary, William Theodore and Tu Weiming, eds, *Confucianism and Human Rights*. New York: Columbia University Press, 1998.

Ding, Yijiang, *Chinese Democracy after Tiananmen Square*. Vancouver and Toronto: UBC Press, 2001.

Gilley, Bruce, *China's Democratic Future*. New York: Columbia University Press, 2004.

He Baogang, *The Democratization of China*. London and New York: Routledge, 1996.

Howell, Jude, ed., *Governance in China*. Lanham, Boulder and New York: Rowman & Littlefield, 2004.

Information Office, State Council, *Building Political Democracy in China*, 2005, http://www.china.org.cn/english/2005/Oct/145718.htm

Information Office, State Council, *China's Efforts and Achievements in Promoting the Rule of Law*, http://www.china.org.cn/en/governmehnt/news/2008-03/28/content_11025486.htm

Information Office, State Council, *White Papers of the Chinese Government*, vols 1–4. Beijing: Foreign Languages Press, 2000, 2002, 2005.

Jiang Jinsong, *The National People's Congress of China*. Beijing: Foreign Languages Press, 2003.

Keith, Ronald C., *China's Struggle for the Rule of Law*. New York and London: St Martin's Press and Macmillan Press, 1994.

Keith, Ronald C. and Zhiqiu Lin, *Law and Justice in China's New Marketplace*. London and New York: Palgrave, 2001.

Keith, Ronald C. and Zhiqqiu Lin, *New Crime in China: Public Order and Human Rights*. London and New York: Routledge, 2006.

Li Buyun, *Constitutionalism and China (Xianzheng yu Zhongguo)*, trans. Huang Lie. Beijing: Falu chubanshe, 2006 (English and Chinese texts).

Lieberthan, Kenneth, *Governing China: From Revolution Through Reform*. New York: W.W. Norton & Co., 1995.

Lin, Chris X., 'A Quiet Revolution: An Overview of China's Judicial Reform', *Asia-Pacific Law and Policy Journal*, vol. 4, no. 2, Summer 2003, pp. 255–319.

Peerenboom, 'Assessing Human Rights in China: Why the Double Standard?', *Cornell International Law Journal*, vol. 71, 2005, pp. 72–162.

Zhao Suisheng, ed., *China and Democracy: Reconsidering the Prospects for a Democratic China*. New York and London: Routledge, 2000.

Socialism or Capitalism with 'Chinese Characteristics'

Deng Xiaoping, *Selected Works of Deng Xiaoping (1975–82)*. Beijing: Foreign Languages Press, 1984.
Deng Xiaoping, *Fundamental Issues in Present Day China*. Beijing: Foreign Languages Press, 1987.
Deng Xiaoping, *Selected Works of Deng Xiaoping (1938–65)*. Beijing Foreign Languages Press, 1992.
Deng Xiaoping, *Selected Works of Deng Xiaoping*, vol. iii (1982–92). Beijing: Foreign Languages Press, 1994.
Dickson, Bruce J., *Wealth into Power: The Communist Party's Embrace of China's Private Sector*. Cambridge and New York: Cambridge University Press, 2008.
Gabriel, Saryananda, *Chinese Capitalism and the Modernist Vision*. London and New York, 2006.
Gittings, John, *The Changing Face of China: From Mao to Market*. Oxford: Oxford University Press, 2005.
Lee, John, *Will China Fail? The Limits and Contradictions of Market Socialism*. St Leonards, NSW: The Centre for Independent Studies Ltd, 2007.
Meisner, Marucie, *The Deng Xiaoping Era: An Inquiry into the Fate of Chinese Socialism 1978–1994*. New York: Hill and Wang, 1996.
Naughton, Barry, *Growing out of the Plan: Chinese Economic Reform 1978–1993*. Cambridge, Mass. and New York: Cambridge University Press, 1996.
Naughton, Barry, *The Chinese Economy: Transitions and Growth*. Cambridge, Mass.: MIT Press, 2007.
Solinger, Dorothy, *China's Transition from Socialism: Statist Legacies and Market Reforms 1980–1990*. Armonk, New York and London: M.E. Sharpe, 1993.
Xue Muqiao, *China's Socialist Economy*. Beijing: Foreign Languages Press, 1981.

New 'Model' for International Relations

Information Office, State Council, *China's Peaceful Development Road*, http://www.china.org.cn/English/20005/Dec/152669.htm
Keith, Ronald C., ed., *China as a Rising World Power and Its Response to 'Globalization'*. London and New York: Routledge, 2005.

Peerenboom, Randall, *China Modernizes: Threat to the West or Model for the Rest*. Oxford: Oxford University Press, 2007.

Wu Guoguang, and Helen Lansdowne, eds, *China Turns to Multilateralism: Foreign Policy and Regional Security*. New York: Routledge, 2008.

Yong Deng, *China's Struggle for Status: The Realignment of International Relations*. Cambridge and New York: Cambridge University Press, 2008.

Zhang Yongjin, *China in International Society since 1949: Alienation and Beyond*. London and New York: Macmillan Press and St Martin's Press, 1998.

China Redux

Chao Chien-min and Bruce Dickson, eds, *Remaking the Chinese State: Strategies, Society and Security*. London and New York: Routledge, 2001.

Documents of the 16th National Congress of the Communist Party of China (2002). Beijing: Foreign Languages Press, 2002.

Documents of the 17th National Congress of the Communist Party of China (2007). Beijing: Foreign Languages Press, 2007.

Fewsmith, Joseph, *China Since Tiananmen: From Deng Xiaoping to Hu Jintao*. New York: Cambridge University Press, 2008.

Keith, Ronald C., ed., *China as a Rising World Power and its Response to 'Globalization'*. London and New York: Routledge, 2005.

Lam, Will Wo-Lap, *Chinese Politics in the Hu Jintao Era: New Leaders, New Challenges*. Armonk and London: M.E. Sharpe, 2006.

Lampton, David M., *The Three Faces of Chinese Power: Might, Money and Minds*. Berkeley, Los Angeles and London: University of California Press, 2008.

O'Brien, Kevin J. and Liangjiang Li, *Rightful Resistance in Rural China*. Cambridge and New York: Cambridge University Press, 2006.

Zweig, David, *Internationalizing China: Domestic Interests and Global Linkages*. Ithaca and London: Cornell University Press, 2002.

INDEX